Roy Lichtenstein

Interiors

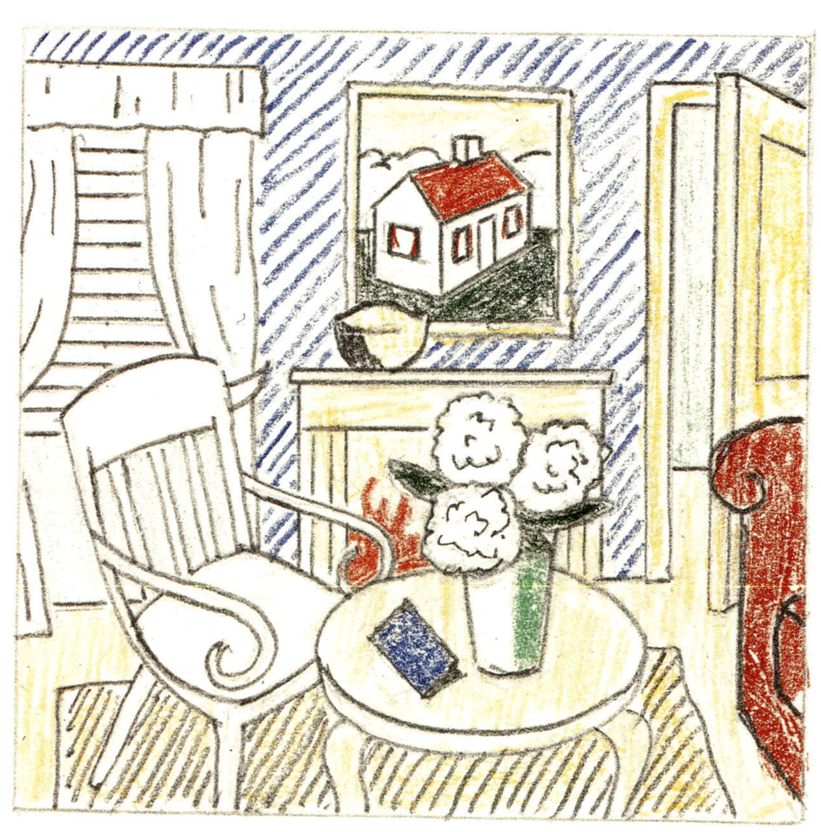

Robert Fitzpatrick
Dorothy Lichtenstein
Leo Castelli
Cassandra Lozano
Sidney B. Felsen

Roy Lichtenstein
Interiors

Hudson Hills Press,
New York,
in association with
Museum of
Contemporary Art,
Chicago

Published in the United States by
Hudson Hills Press, Inc.
1133 Broadway, Suite 1301
New York, NY 10010-8001

Editor and Publisher
Paul Anbinder

Distributed in the United States, its territories and possessions, and Canada by National Book Network.

Distributed in the United Kingdom, Eire, and Europe by Windsor Books International.

Unless otherwise indicated in the captions, photography credits are provided on page 102.

Produced by the Publications Department of the Museum of Contemporary Art, Chicago. Designed and typeset by Hal Kugeler, Director of Design and Publications. Edited by Michael Sittenfeld, Associate Director of Publications, with the assistance of Kari Dahlgren, Editor.

This book was initially published in conjunction with the exhibition *Roy Lichtenstein: Interiors* held at the Museum of Contemporary Art, Chicago, from July 24 to October 10, 1999.

The exhibition *Roy Lichtenstein: Interiors* was generously sponsored by the Sara Lee Foundation and the Northern Trust Corporation.

Exhibition Curators
Robert Fitzpatrick and Dorothy Lichtenstein

Assistant Curators
Cassandra Lozano and Michael Rooks

Printed by Cantz in Germany

Color separations by Professional Graphics in Rockford, Illinois

Library of Congress Card Number: 00-109000

ISBN 1-555-95-205-4

COVER
Nude with Yellow Flower, 1994. Cat. no. 48.

FRONTISPIECE
Interior with Bouquet, 1997. Cat. no. 62.

BACK COVER
Clipping from Lichtenstein scrapbook (*Girls' Love Stories*, no. 97 © 1963 DC Comics).

Contents

9 Sponsors' Statements

10 Foreword
Robert Fitzpatrick

13 Perfect Pictures
Robert Fitzpatrick

19 The Misanthrope Manqué: Through a Glass Lightly
Dorothy Lichtenstein

23 Framing George
Leo Castelli

25 Words and Pictures
Cassandra Lozano

29 Roy
Sidney B. Felsen

33 Plates

85 The Interior Prints

96 Selected Bibliography

97 Exhibition Checklist

101 Lenders to the Exhibition

102 Notes on Contributors

102 Photography Credits

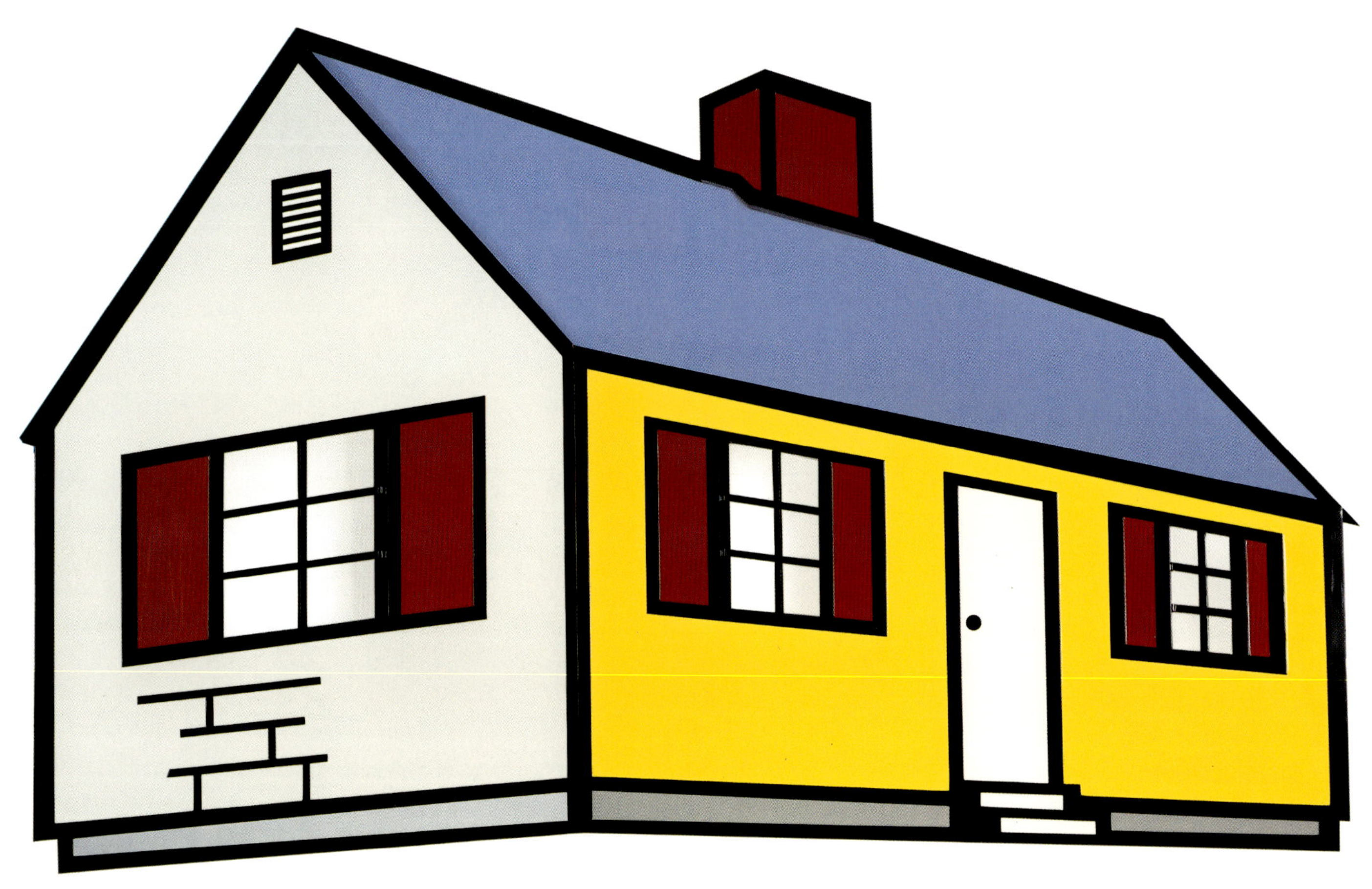

Sponsors' Statements

The **Sara Lee Foundation** is pleased to join the Museum of Contemporary Art in presenting this exhibition exploring the vision of a major American artist.

The work of Roy Lichtenstein compels us to question our experiences of art and contemporary life. *Roy Lichtenstein: Interiors* provides a unique opportunity for us to consider the artist's work.

Sara Lee Corporation has encouraged and supported cultural endeavors throughout the world for nearly sixty years, particularly in our headquarters city of Chicago. Please join me in celebrating the work of Roy Lichtenstein.

C. STEVEN MCMILLAN
President and
Chief Operating Officer
Sara Lee Corporation

Northern Trust Corporation is delighted to support its friends at the Museum of Contemporary Art in presenting *Roy Lichtenstein: Interiors*, an exhibition that offers audiences a comprehensive yet intimate look at the work of this important twentieth-century artist. Roy Lichtenstein has influenced the work of many artists, and the breadth of his accomplishments has intrigued audiences for decades.

We invite you to join the Northern Trust Corporation in recognizing the achievements of Roy Lichtenstein through this outstanding exhibition at the Museum of Contemporary Art.

BARRY G. HASTINGS
President and
Chief Operating Officer
Northern Trust Corporation

House I, 1997.
Polyurethane and Magna on aluminum;
179 × 122 1/2 × 54 1/4 in.
Private collection, New York.

Foreword

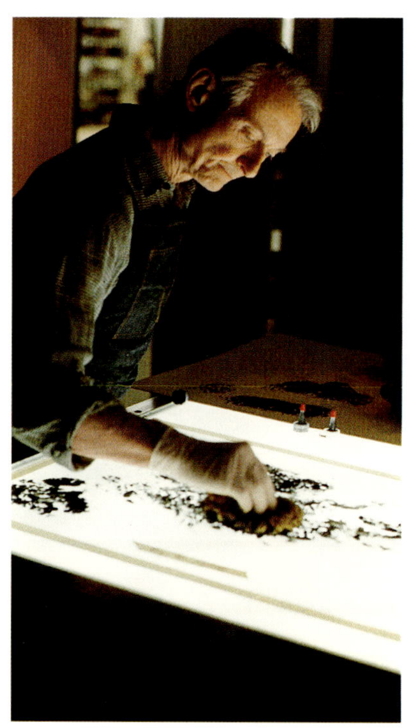

Roy Lichtenstein working on the *Interior* series at Gemini G.E.L., February 1990. Photograph © Sidney B. Felsen 1990.

IN 1977, AS THE NEW President of Cal Arts, I wanted to mount an exhibition for young artists that explored the moment of creative birth, the moment when an idea becomes a work of art. I went to see Roy and Dorothy Lichtenstein in Southhampton, and asked Roy if we could do an exhibition of his drawings and collages — works that would offer insights into the creative process and that showed clear traces of the artist's hand.

Roy agreed, and suggested that we invite Allan Kaprow, a former Cal Arts faculty member and colleague at Rutgers, to curate the exhibition. It was put together around the Lichtensteins' kitchen table. The result was very moving for the young artists for whom it was intended.

Twenty-two years later, I became Director of the Museum of Contemporary Art. Bill Cook, the Associate Director of the museum, suggested that Dorothy Lichtenstein and I curate an exhibition of Roy's interiors. Thus, this project was born.

In this exhibition, we present Lichtenstein's source materials to convey the moments in which he conceived his paintings, sculptures, drawings, and works on paper. We hope readers and visitors will share the artist's sense of discovery as he sifted through comic books, yellow pages, and other sources. The catalogue's essays present an intimate portrait of the artist through the voices of those who knew him best. They offer insights into his personality, ideas, and working methods, and celebrate his generosity and his vaunted sense of humor.

It is with tremendous appreciation that I acknowledge the generous funding provided by the Sara Lee Foundation and the Northern Trust Corporation for *Roy Lichtenstein: Interiors.* These organizations have given the public a rare chance to understand the working process of a great artist.

I am deeply grateful to all who have given assistance and support to this exhibition, particularly Bill Cook, who died before it could be realized.

I am indebted to Larry Gagosian for his enthusiasm and

extraordinary help, and I am grateful for the generosity of all the lenders, whose great fondness for Roy as an artist and friend encouraged their participation.

Many of my colleagues at the MCA have been involved in the exhibition. I am thankful to Don Meckley and the preparators for an outstanding installation, and to Jennifer Draffen and Meredith Gray for their registrarial work. Special thanks are due to Hal Kugeler for the design of this catalogue and to Michael Sittenfeld for editing this volume. I also wish to thank Leo Castelli, Sidney Felsen, Cassandra Lozano, and Dorothy Lichtenstein for their contributions to the catalogue.

I am deeply indebted to Assistant Curator Michael Rooks, whose scholarship, mastery of logistics, and diplomatic skills were crucial to every aspect of this project, and to Cassandra Lozano of the Lichtenstein Foundation, whose assistance and advice was indispensable. I also owe many thanks to Etienne Dufay for designing the exhibition. Without their efforts, *Roy Lichtenstein: Interiors* could not have been realized.

Finally, I am profoundly grateful to Dorothy Lichtenstein for co-curating this exhibition, and for offering her friendship and her time. It has been a tremendous pleasure to work with her and to revisit Roy's life and career.

ROBERT FITZPATRICK
Director
Museum of Contemporary Art, Chicago

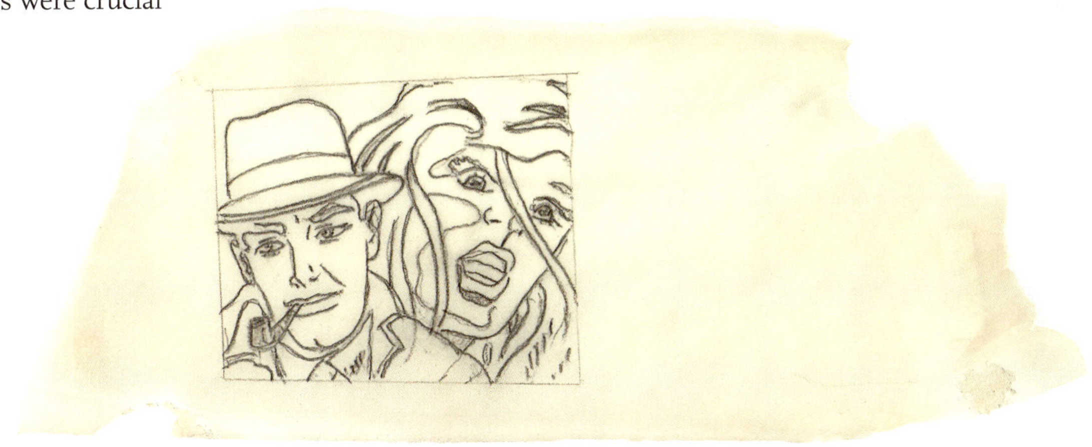

Large Interior with Three Reflections (sketch for painting), 1993. Cat. no. 43.

Titles in bold indicate works in the exhibition.

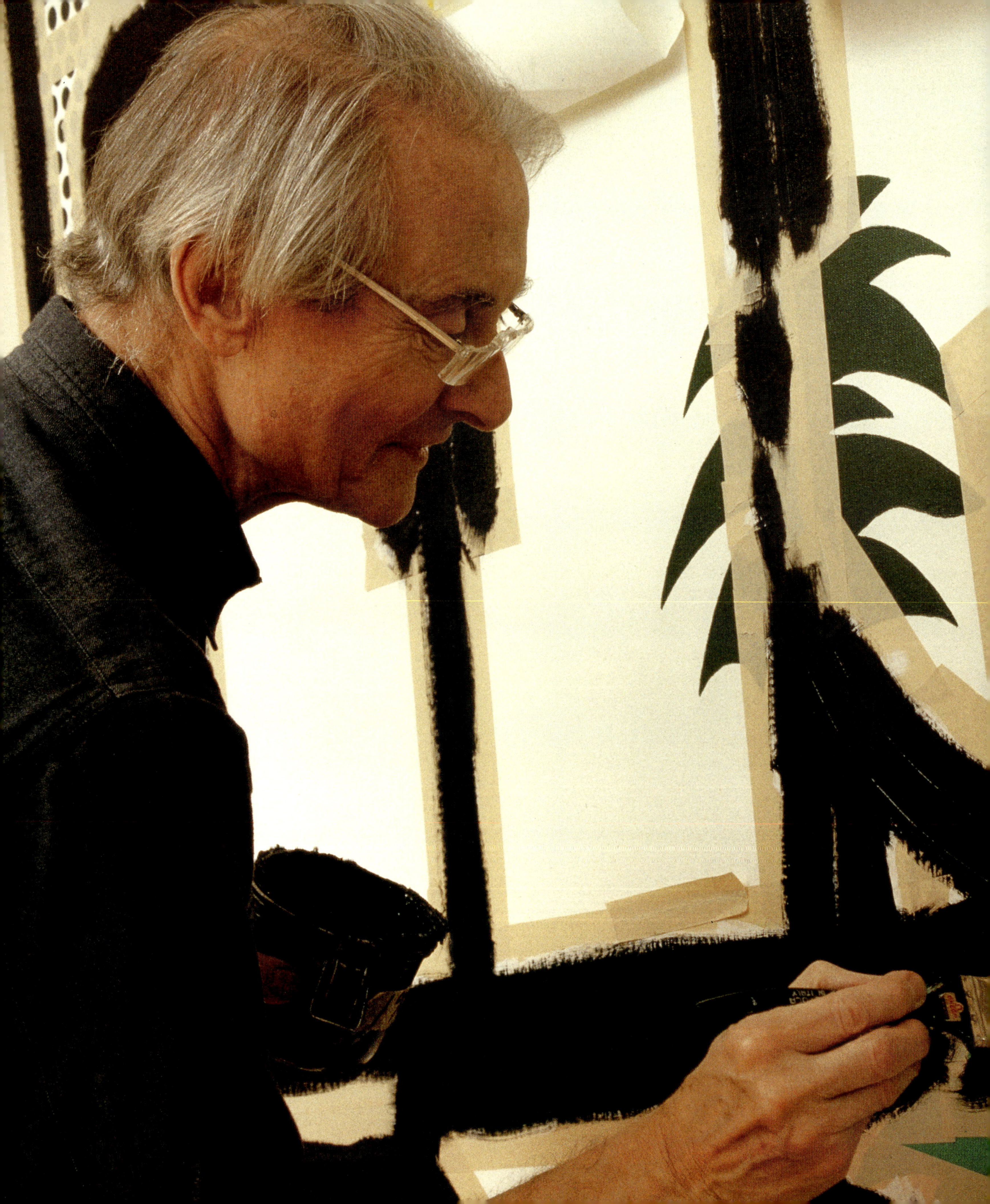

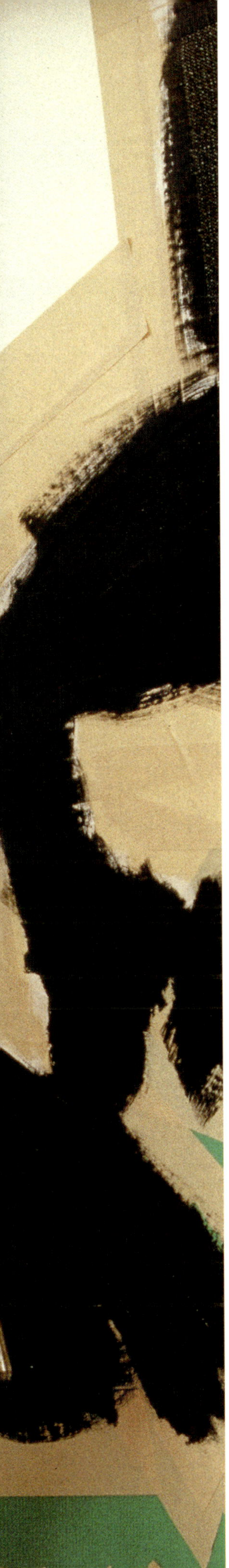

Perfect Pictures

Robert Fitzpatrick

Roy Lichtenstein at his Southhampton studio in 1992. Photograph © Bob Adelman.

Roy Lichtenstein's wit inspirited his art. Nowhere is this more apparent than in his interior works, which bristle with irony and the artist's sharp sense of humor. As the first large body of work that Lichtenstein started in the 1990s, the interiors caricatured the excessive 1980s documented in colorful spreads of art-filled interiors in magazines like *Architectural Digest*. Yet they may also be understood in relation to British Pop artist Richard Hamilton's collage spoofing the ideal modern interiors of the 1950s, *Just what is it that makes today's homes so different, so appealing?* (1956; see p. 14), often regarded as the image that ushered in Pop Art as a major international movement. Hamilton's interior, decked out with modern conveniences such as a television set and a vacuum cleaner, anticipated Lichtenstein's much later interiors. This is especially evident in Hamilton's use of a "cheesecake" photo from a "girlie" magazine, which prefigures Lichtenstein's nudes culled from the pages of romance comic books.

Solitary and unlived in, the interiors represent domestic settings in which daily life and private acts can only be imagined. There is no clutter, no human presence — even the occasional nude seems to adorn rather than inhabit the space. Lichtenstein called the interiors "bland" and "inhuman" and he enjoyed playing with their simplicity while making something sophisticated of them. He took particular delight in magnifying small advertisements to life-size proportions, revealing the folly of domestic conventions that alternately inspire and reflect these lifeless images.

Lichtenstein was interested in the interior as a subject as early as 1961. In drawings from that year, such as *Bathroom, Curtains,* and *Couch* (see p. 15) he extracted elements from household surroundings and translated them into simple graphic shapes. Some of these later emerged in his earliest interiors such as *Artist's Studio: Foot Medication* (1974; Stefan T. Edlis Collection, Chicago), in which the skirted sofa is shown partially concealed behind a stack of paintings.

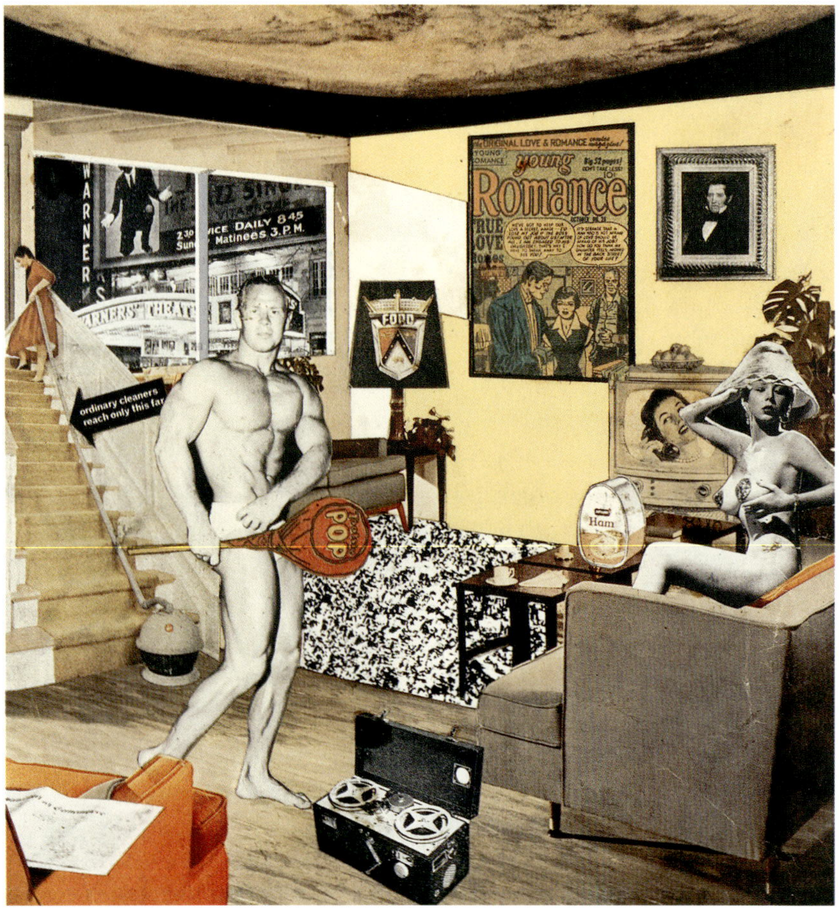

Richard Hamilton (British, b. 1922). *Just what is it that makes today's homes so different, so appealing?*, 1956. Collage on paper; 10 1/4 × 9 3/4 in. © 2001 Artists Rights Society (ARS), New York/DACS, London. Photo courtesy of Anthony d'Offay Gallery, London

The interiors were settings in which Lichtenstein's imagination could reinvent the world around him in his particular style and with his brand of humor. For example, the pristine, ultracool interiors that Lichtenstein painted stood in sharp contrast to the cluttered, lived-in spaces of his studio. His process of invention was a fluid give-and-take, continually modifying and refining his own images in the spirit of play rather than work, but serious play—he always took art seriously but he would never take himself seriously at all. The capacity of Lichtenstein's art to engage such dualities — whimsy and complexity, drollery and sophistication, parody and reverence — enlivens his work and is a continual source of pleasure.

Within the interiors, Lichtenstein lampoons his own art as well as that of others. Yet his allusions and appropriations never mock or condescend. They provoke a wry smile, one perhaps similar to the gleeful expression in his eyes that accompanied the slightest beginnings of a wicked grin. More often than not, his humor was directed at himself. Many of his own works appear on the walls of the interiors, but are stylized — Lichtenstein's versions of Lichtensteins, just as his earlier take-offs on Picasso's paintings are clearly Picasso à la Lichtenstein. In the pristine setting of *Interior with African Mask* (1991; see pp. 72–73), it is not clear whether the oval mirror in the background represents a mirror or the Lichtenstein painting *Oval Mirror 6' × 3' #3* (1973; see p. 19). Because the mirror in the painting is actually painted on canvas, representation and reality become interchangeable — Lichtenstein's own kind of virtual reality.

Similarly, it is uncertain whether the painting hanging on the wall in *Interior with Exterior* (*Still Waters*) (1991; see pp. 62–63) is supposed to represent one of Gilbert Stuart's portraits of George Washington or Lichtenstein's 1962 painting after Stuart (1991; see p. 62). Lichtenstein's reference to the portrait recalls his

1951 painting made in his youthful abstract style after Emanuel Leutze's *Washington Crossing the Delaware* (1897; The Metropolitan Museum of Art, New York). As pendant works in the evolution of Lichtenstein's mature style, characterized by benday dots and the hard-edged look of graphic design, the thick, gestural depiction of water in the earlier painting stands in sharp contrast to the flat, stylized pattern of water in the swimming pool.

With characteristic wit, Lichtenstein even quoted his interiors in the interiors by depicting them in mirrored walls. In the print *Blue Floor* (1991; see p. 88), Lichtenstein extends the perspectival space of the interior in a mirror's "reflection" while allowing the reflection to function also as a painting on the wall. The illusion is especially effective in his life-size version of this print, *Wallpaper with Blue Floor Interior* (1992; see pp. 94–95), which fools the eye into believing for a brief moment that it is an extension of the viewer's actual space. The simulated wood-grain pattern of the floor is prefigured in his painting *Trompe L'oeil with Léger Head and Paintbrush* (1973; see p. 17), a work about illusion deliberately made to look artificial.

Not content with merely reversing an interior in a reflection, Lichtenstein also abstracted it by depicting the mirror image as if distorted by the refractive play of light in the glass of the mirror. A magnificent example of this is his tour de force *Large Interior with Three Reflections* (1993; see pp. 51–52), a mural-size triptych that is reversed and abstracted in a companion triptych representing three large mirrors (see pp. 53–54). It is worth noting that Lichtenstein had a habit of reviewing works in a mirror to make sure that they "read" in reverse and were not unbalanced or disproportionate. So the use of mirrors in his work serves as a self-referential device, suggesting an ironic detachment in the regard of his own painting process.

This inventive playfulness was part of Lichtenstein's genius. With tongue in cheek, he would leave bald-faced clues underscoring his great concern for, and mastery of, formal issues in art, such as the word COMPOSITIONS splayed across the top of his famous 1964 painting *Composition II* (see p. 16). Another example literally sticks out like a sore thumb in *Interior: Perfect Pitcher* (1994; see p. 83). The punning title refers to a still-life painting — a picture of pitchers — on the wall of the interior. A thumb discernible at the bottom edge of the still-life

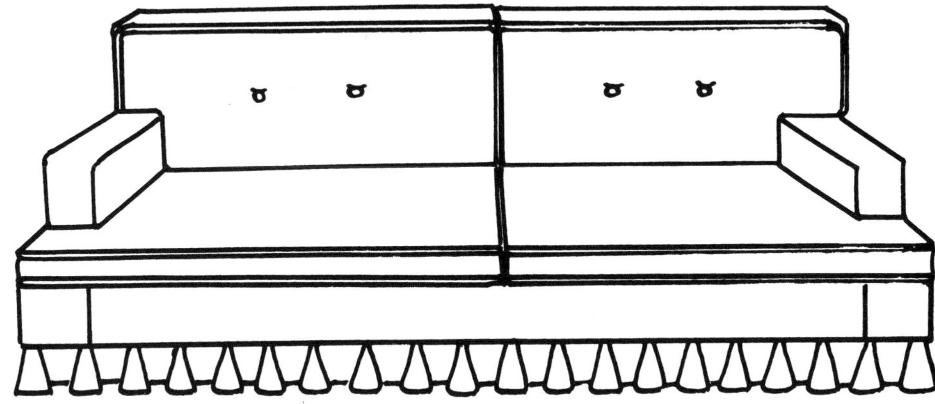

Couch, 1961. Ink on paper; 19 3/4 × 23 1/4 in. Sonnabend Collection, New York.

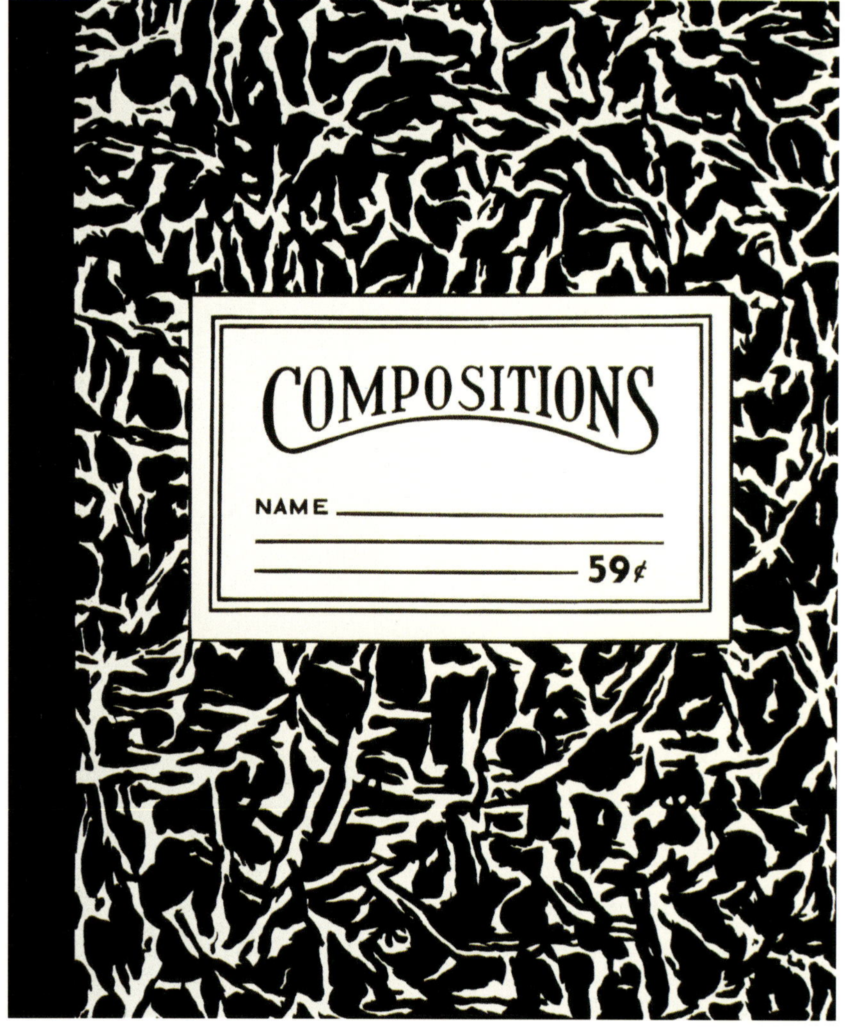

Composition II, 1964.
Oil and Magna
on canvas; 56 × 48 in.
Sonnabend Collection,
New York.

painting is a comic gesture of the artist's final approval of a "perfect" composition. Still another example lies at the very center of the triptych *Large Interior with Three Reflections,* where the word FORM appears in a painting on the wall.

One intention of the present volume is to reveal Lichtenstein's very personal process of collecting and editing source materials from comics, magazines, and telephone book ads, which he then reworked in drawings and collages for larger works. Following the evolution of an image from a scrapbook to an intermediary work to its final realization, we are able to grasp in an intimate way Lichtenstein's working methods and thought processes. These sketchbook studies give one a genuine understanding of his gentleness and his sense of humor, as well as the craftsmanship in his art. On a single page from his "Interiors" scrapbook, three thumbnail sketches nearly the size of postage stamps reveal the beginnings of the large painting *Interior with Bonsai Tree* (1991; see pp. 44–45). With the same economy of means, he transforms a comic book bather into a nude in *Nude with Yellow Flower* (1994; see p. 43), waggishly undressing her, changing her rotary telephone into a cordless one, and replacing the cord in her hand with a daffodil.

Lichtenstein took the nudes off the walls and allowed them to inhabit the interiors, yet they remain as carefully edited and stylized as a sofa, lamp, or throw pillow. These are the perfect inhabitants for Lichtenstein's cool, linear worlds, ironically incongruous in their domestic settings, as are the furnishings themselves. They are not sensuous or even sexy, but objectified to elicit the same response as would an ashtray or potted plant, indicative of Lichtenstein's fondness for elevating the commonplace (telephone book ads) to the extraordinary, and of reducing the extraordinary (nudes) to the commonplace.

Armed with a large variety of source materials, Lichtenstein transformed the media-derived images of the contemporary world into symbols for an almost abstract notion of domesticity — interiors that, as Leo Castelli says in this volume, look uninhabitable. Lichtenstein's interiors are distillations of the types of interiors found in magazines like *Metropolitan Home* or *Architectural Digest* — stylized to a degree of unnatural orderliness, and appealing for that reason. They are worlds minus all the noise and clutter of real life.

The art in Lichtenstein's interiors is similarly reduced to archetypes, things we recognize as Conceptual Art, Abstract Expressionist art, and Pop Art. Even when we recognize specific works such as Warhol's *Flowers* (1966/67) and *Mao* (1972/74), or Robert Motherwell's *Je t'aime No. IV* (1955; see p. 38), these are reduced to symbols for those artists who typify a certain mode or style. Therefore, Lichtenstein's references to his own work are funny and intriguing in this context, acknowledging his role in art history, and reducing his work even further to emblematize a style that is itself emblematic. One may ask when these paintings in the paintings cease being by Roy Lichtenstein, or in turn, whether these paintings in the paintings are themselves autonomous works. Such questioning reveals the underlying complexity of the boundaries between our experiences of art and of contemporary life, boundaries that Lichtenstein's oeuvre has so forcefully led us to reevaluate in the second half of the twentieth century.

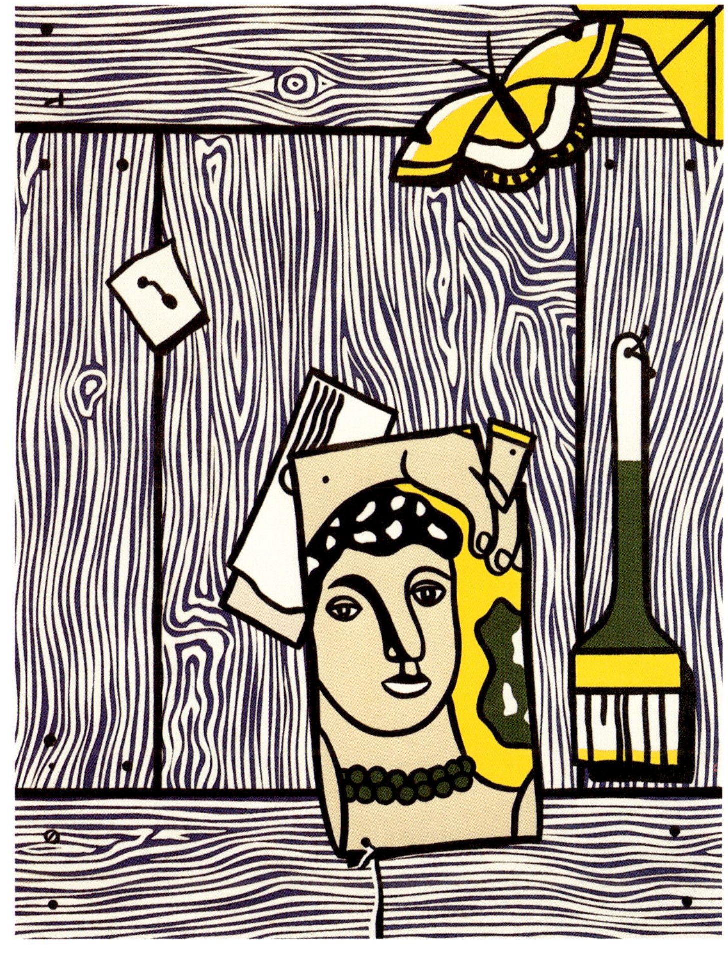

Trompe L'oeil with Léger Head and Paintbrush, 1973. Oil and Magna on canvas; 46 × 36 in. Private collection.

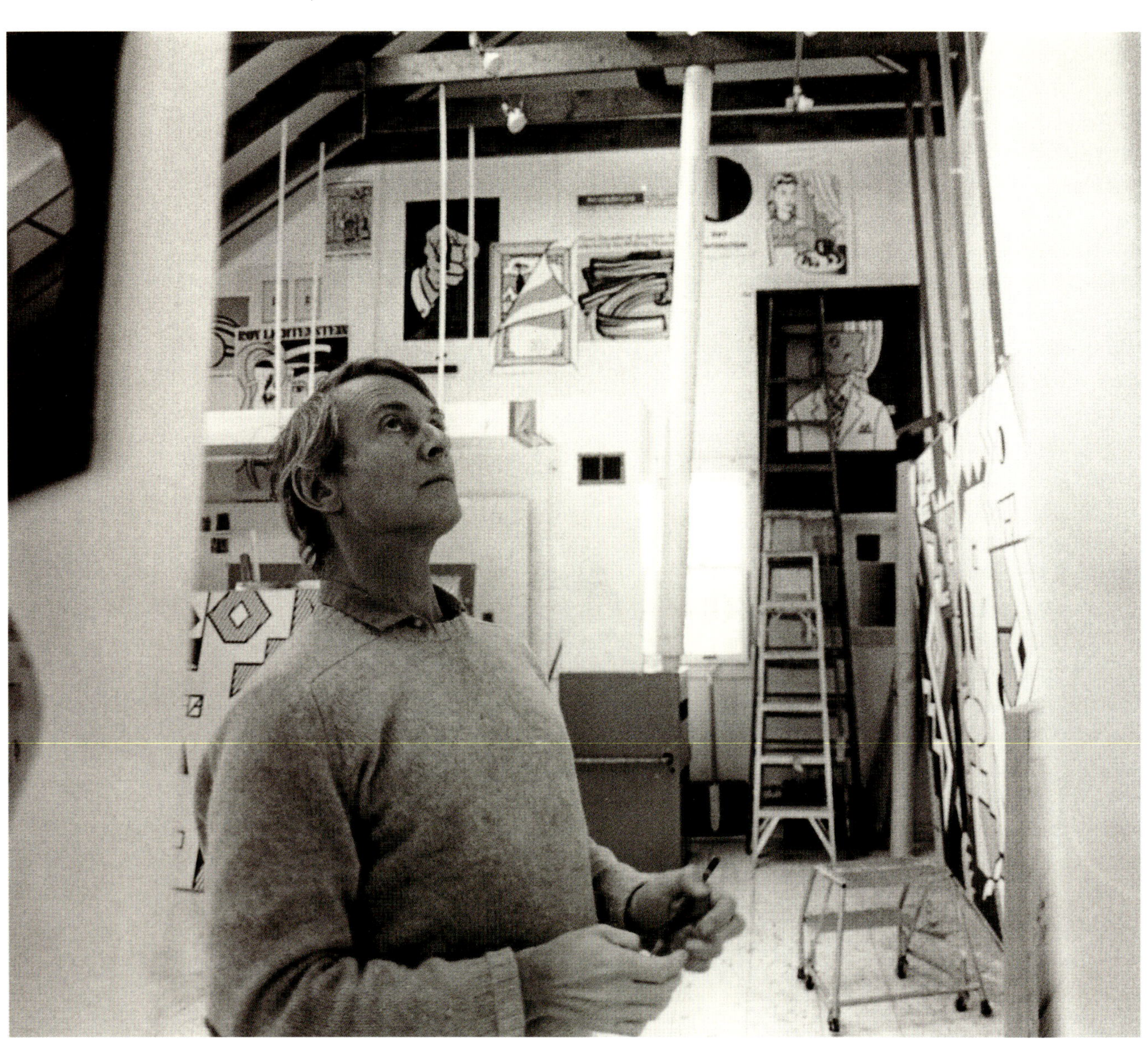

The Misanthrope Manqué: Through a Glass Lightly

Dorothy Lichtenstein

Roy Lichtenstein in his Southampton studio. Photograph © 1979 by Lenore Seroka. Courtesy Estate of Roy Lichtenstein.

Oval Mirror 6' × 3' #3, 1971. Cat. no. 3.

THE INTERIOR OF ROY'S STUDIO in Southampton, where he worked from 1970 on, had grown into a friendly and comfortable clutter of miscellany. The hodgepodge included paper coffee cups embellished with Greek columns; advertising imagery representing the perfect apple, banana, grapefruit; his somewhat desecrated collection of comics worn thin from use; tattered art books, their pages dog-eared throughout. Collated combinations of colored, dotted, and striped scraps of paper were taped to every surface. The upper walls of the barnlike structure were plastered with his posters. Pencils, protractors, single-edged razor blades, surgical scalpels, tongue depressors, guitar picks, perforated sheets of paper, every width of masking tape known to man . . . these tools of the trade spilled across his work table. A large assortment of Ball jars and coffee cans containing paint and turpentine lined the shelves. Maps and charts were tacked to the walls, as was a periodic chart of the elements complete with atomic data. There were definitions of elementary particles (those elusive quarks and neutrinos he pondered) hanging everywhere.

Scientific rationalist though he was, Roy also had great fondness for the pseudoscientific. Among his favorites was a fading tabloid headline: "You can call the dead . . . Collect!!!" His enjoyment of irony (he planned to leave his soul to science) is easily inferred from his early parodies of American historical painting to his late interiors. The exhibition *Roy Lichtenstein: Interiors* is a perfect representation of the man and his method of working. Not that Roy would have dreamed of living in any of these rooms, with their appalling approximation of bromidic bad taste, prototypical platitudinousness, and flattened furnishings. No doubt he would laugh at my harebrained attempt with idiotically inspired, overly onomatopoeic, similar sounding syllables to describe his own sweet, straight-shooting self.

Roy saw through a glass lightly. He worked and played with this vision as his guiding light, an inner compass. He was "all of a piece," and to see him in his natural habitat, the studio, or playpen, as he liked to call it, was to witness continuity/congruity/coherence. Inspiration was everywhere: the aforementioned coffee cup, the images of ideal blondes, fearless heroes, reddest apples were all grist for the mill. His view of a painting obscured by the play of reflections on its protective glass provided him with a wealth of ideas. Are we looking at the reflection of a window in a mirror or through the window itself? Is that a mirror of a painting or a painting of a mirror? Or as Roy might say, only marks on canvas, a group of artfully placed lines and shapes symbolizing mirrorness? Are we outside looking in, or inside looking out? Is that an "imperfect" sculpture of an "imperfect" painting I see before me? Which came first? And what about that perfect "pitcher"?

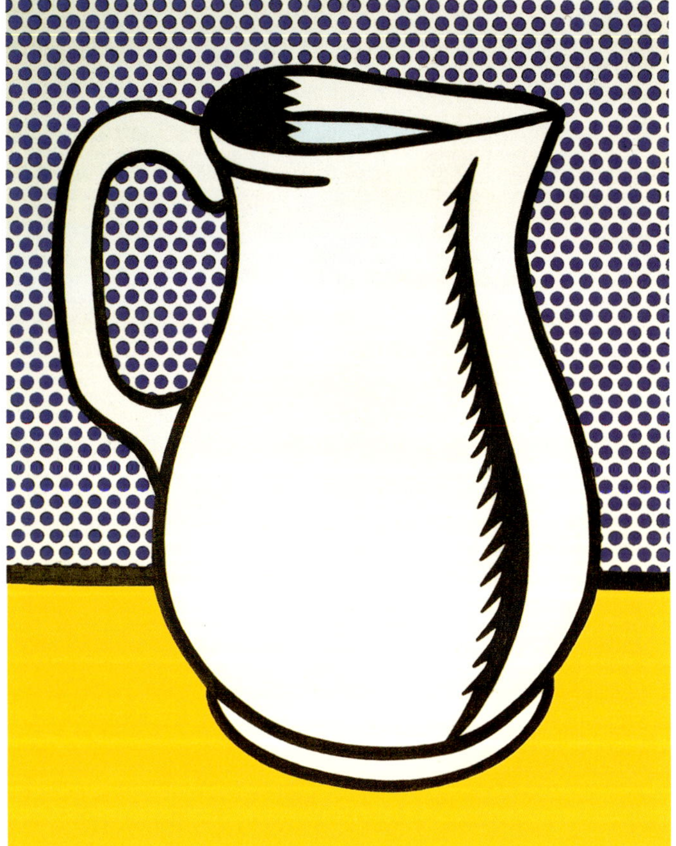

Pitcher Triptych, 1972.
Cat. no. 5.

Roy loved music and the studio was always filled with the sounds he loved. Bach and bebop were his favorites. He always kept his flute handy (the last few years he struggled with a saxophone), ready to join the sounds he surrounded himself with. And wouldn't you know, those musical notes found their way into his paintings.

Though he was somewhat shy, Roy's curiosity made him open and friendly. Sentimentality was as foreign to him as humanitarianism was natural. He claimed his failure to carry a grudge was due to poor memory. It wasn't that he was above the rest of our nefarious inclinations. He could be cunning and devilish indeed, but the sense of gratitude he felt for his own good fortune permeated his daily life and made him a kind and reverent man.

He had such trouble saying no that he contemplated signing up for curmudgeon lessons. How lucky for us the class was filled!

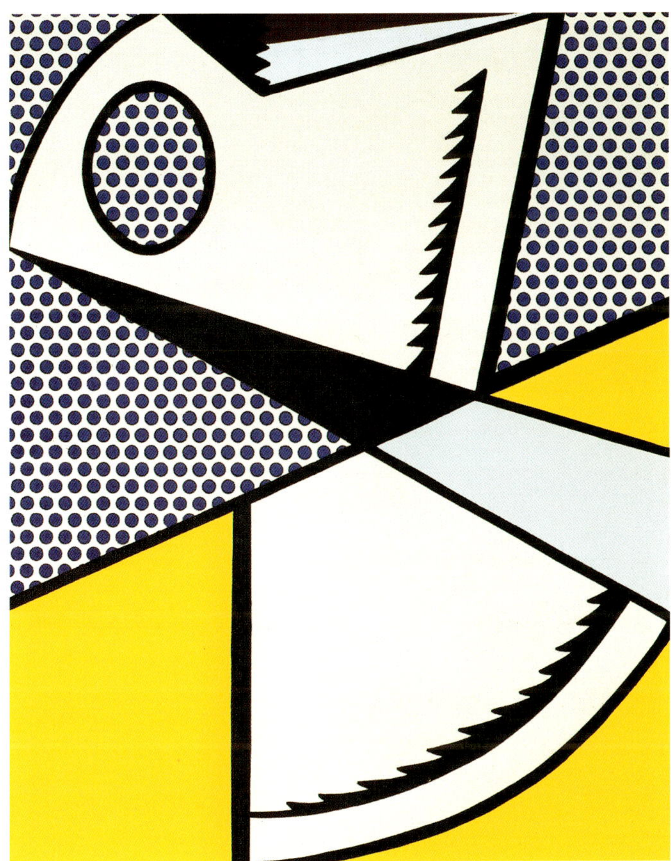

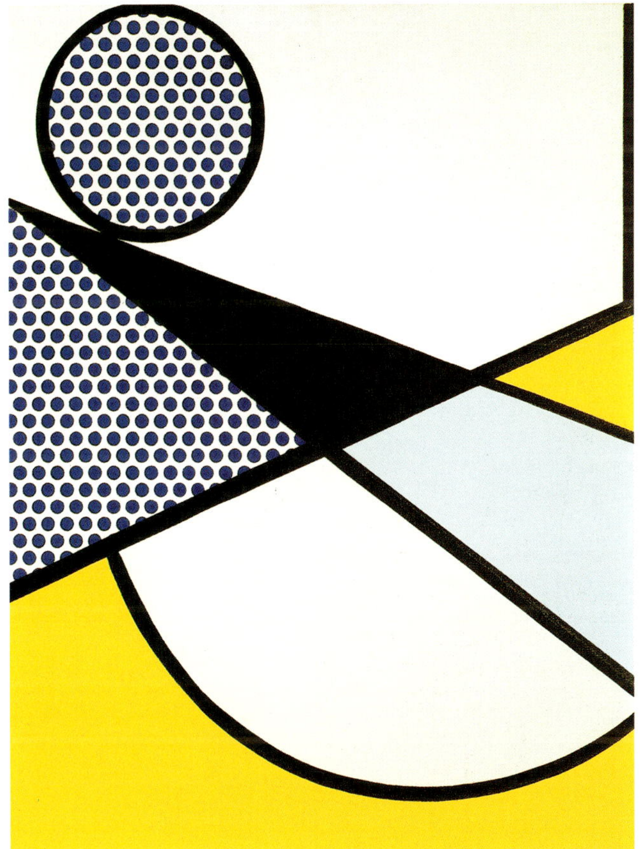

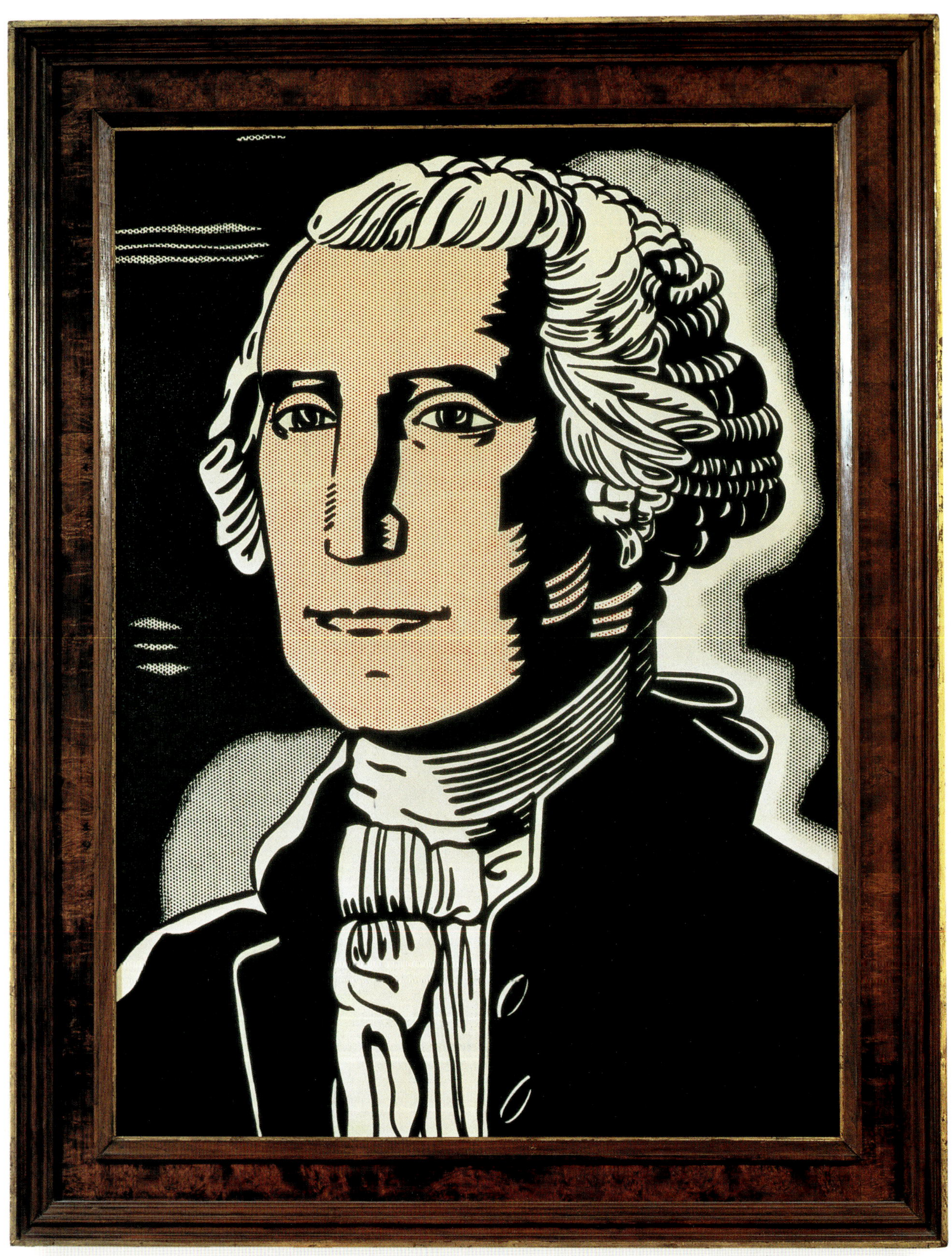

Framing George

Leo Castelli

LEFT
George Washington, 1962. Cat. no. 1.

Leo Castelli and Roy Lichtenstein standing in front of *Interior with Yves Klein Sculpture* (1991). Photograph by Robert McKeever. © Estate of Roy Lichtenstein.

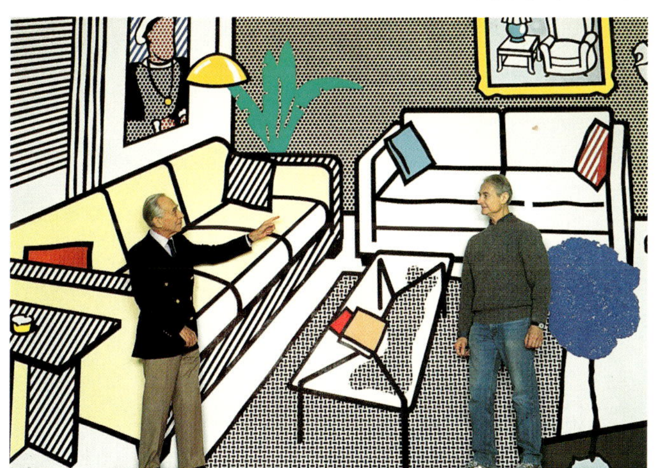

One day Roy Lichtenstein asked me if I had an important frame I could give him. He intended to paint something for which a special frame seemed necessary. I happened to have one that I thought would fulfill his wishes. This frame once belonged to a Dubuffet painting and it was so imposing that I had to remove it in order to be able to sell the painting. Roy had found what he was looking for and took it.

The painting that he made for this frame turned out to be his well-known portrait *George Washington,* and of course, when I first saw it, I knew that my frame was a perfect match for this special subject. This would not be the last time Roy would suprise me with one of his inventions.

For many years, when Roy worked on a new group of paintings, the result always surprised me. It was a surprise to see *George Washington* hanging on the wall in one of his interiors in the early nineties. By then I had bought *George Washington,* and for the moment it was hanging on one of the walls of my apartment. Looking at *Interior with Exterior* (*Still Waters*) (1991; see pp. 62–63), I asked myself if Roy wasn't actually painting the interior of my apartment. But the only thing that I was familiar with in the room depicted in the painting was my own Lichtenstein.

What I see when I stand in front of any interior of Roy's is a work of an important artist that I immediately recognize: a Calder, a blue sponge sculpture by Yves Klein, a Lichtenstein, a Johns from the late eighties. But if you eliminate these works from the interiors, they become unreal. They are too perfect. The environment is too clean to be habitable.

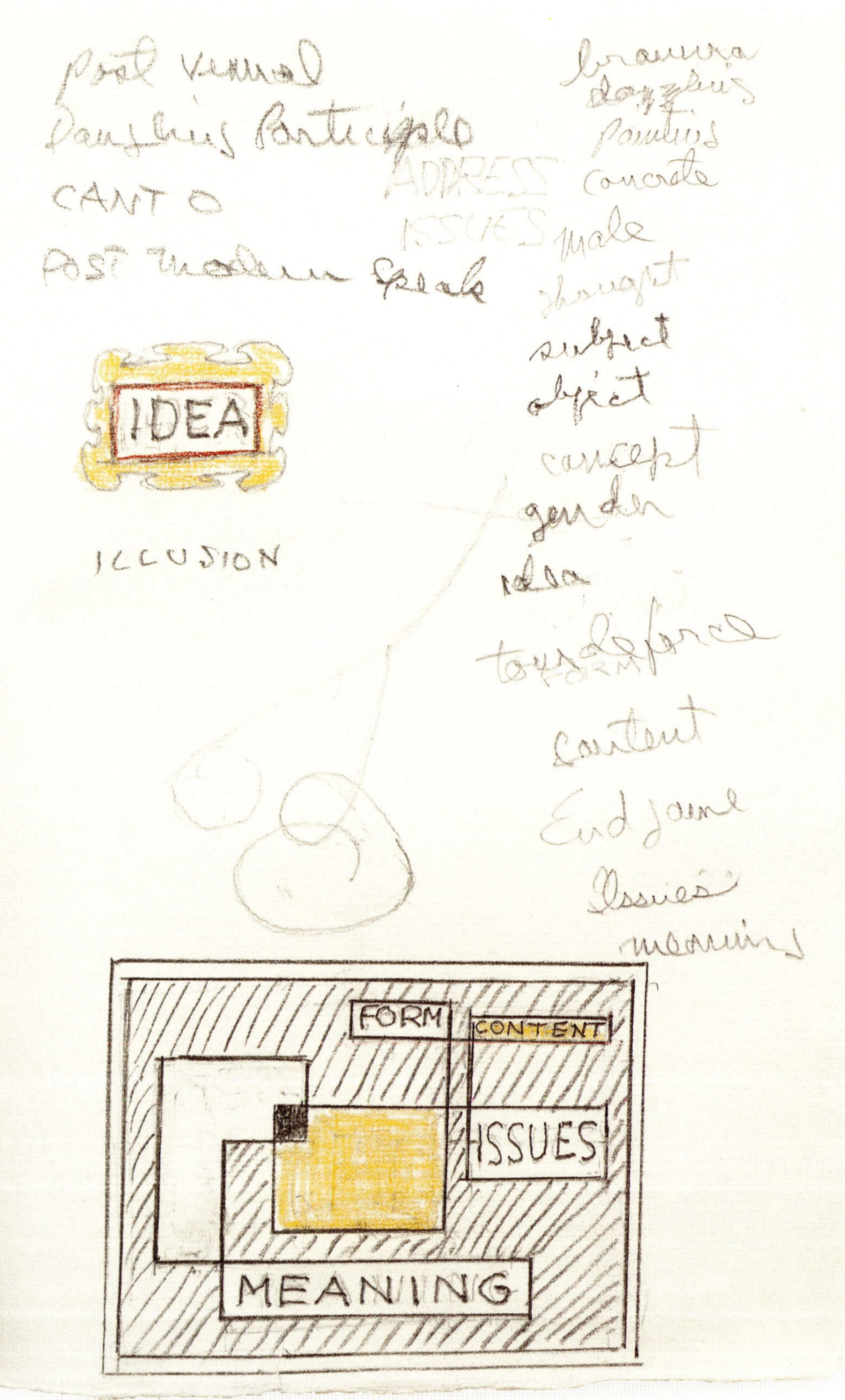

Post visual
Dangling Participle
CANT O
Post modern speak
ADDRESS
ISSUES
bravura
dazzling
painting
concrete
male
thought
subject
object
concept
gender
idea
tour de force
FORM
content
End game
Issues
meaning
IDEA
ILLUSION
FORM
CONTENT
ISSUES
MEANING

Words and Pictures

Cassandra Lozano

LEFT
Idea (sketch for painting), 1993. Cat. no. 36.

Post Visual, 1993. Oil and Magna on canvas; 96 × 80 in. Private collection.

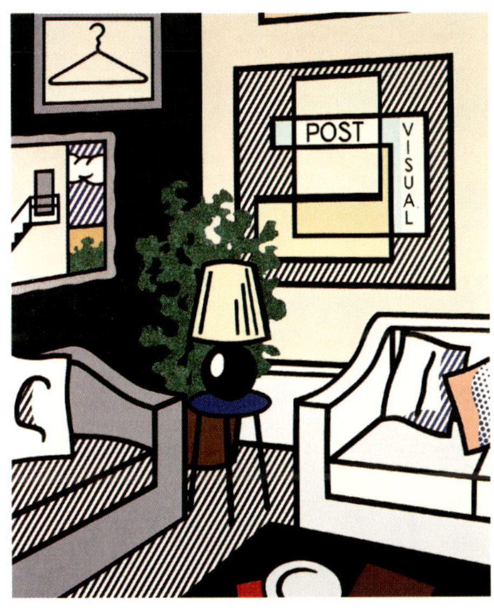

Roy Lichtenstein had two studios: one in New York City and one in Southampton. The studio in New York was twice as big as the Southampton space, with twice as many work tables and sculpture stands. Each studio had a floor-to-ceiling easel system, which held work of any shape or size, and rotating easels of Lichtenstein's own design that allowed him to work on his paintings upside down. He constantly rotated the paintings as he worked on them, for convenience and to appreciate their abstract qualities. Each studio also had a mirror that he would place in front of his paintings to see if a composition was pleasing in reverse.

Roy had his own system of premixed colors. The paints, organized by color, were on shelves, and by each set of shelves was a paint chart listing all Lichtensteinian colors standardized for both studios. The brushes, pencils, and everything else had its place. There was rarely a drop of paint on the floor.

The studios were designed for making art. There was beauty in their simplicity. They were large and airy, with art, plants, and pieces of well-chosen furniture. In the early 1970s, Roy made a series of works inspired by Henri Matisse's painting *The Red Studio* (1911; The Museum of Modern Art, New York) that evoke the feeling of Matisse's canvas as well as they capture the spirit of Lichtenstein's studio. In the lower right corner of the study for Lichtenstein's *The Artist's Studio with Model* (1974; see p. 26) we literally see Roy's hand drawing a sketch of a veiled dancer in the style of Matisse. In the painting, works by Lichtenstein line the wall of the studio, with an "explosion" sculpture appearing on the left behind the dancer and an "entablature" painting hanging on the back wall. To the right are two images: a precursor to Lichtenstein's "perfect" and "imperfect" paintings of 1985–88; and the "man with pipe," which shows up as a detail in *Large Interior with Three Reflections* (1993; see pp. 51–54). Matissesque foliage and still-life objects enliven the scene. The studio depicted is full of clues to Lichtenstein's art —

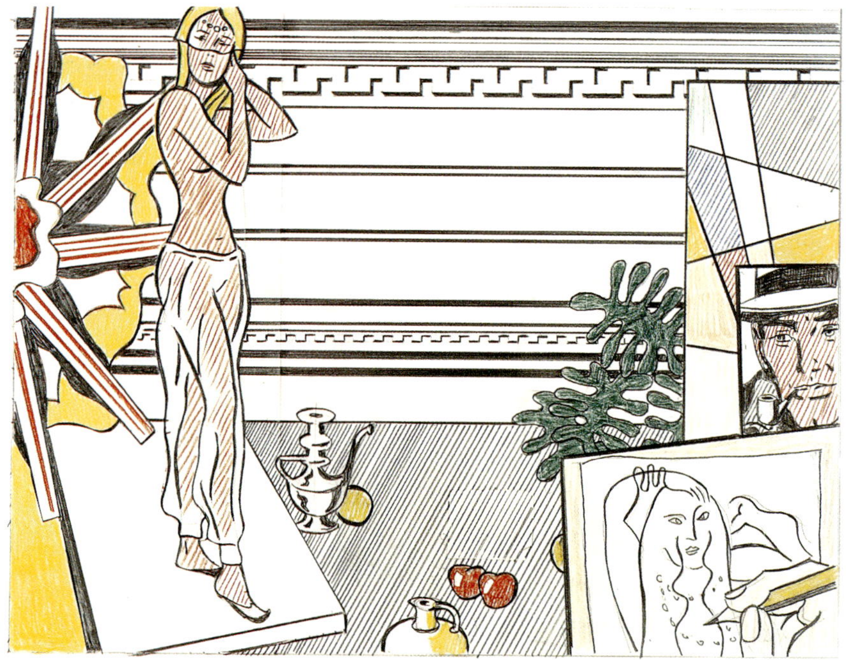

Artist's Studio: Model (drawing for painting), 1974. Cat. no. 6.

previous ideas he could not part with and new ideas he tucked away for future use.

Roy never wanted to leave the studio. He often worked seven days a week and did not like to travel, but in 1989 Roy lived in Rome as an artist-in-residence at the American Academy. While he enjoyed Rome, the distractions of the city interfered with his habitual need to be in the studio working. He found inspiration not in the museums, piazzas, or the Roman Forum, but in billboards and the yellow pages. He cut out images of bedrooms, kitchens, and living rooms from the phone book and pasted them into the "composition" notebooks in which he gathered his images for future use. These images became the basis of the interior works of 1991–97. Reminiscent of the stark banality of Lichtenstein's *Bathroom* (1961; Mr. and Mrs. S. I. Newhouse Jr. Collection, New York), the interior paintings portray upper-middle-class living rooms overstuffed with furniture and fine art of uncertain provenance. The consumer society that Lichtenstein depicted in his Pop paintings of the sixties became, in his nineties interiors, a world of consumer excess.

In targeting the lifestyle of much of the museumgoing public, Lichtenstein's interiors are more ironic than the playfully autobiographical studio paintings. But his use of irony in the interiors goes well beyond satirizing consumerism. This is evident in his incorporation of words in the paintings. Lichtenstein loved the rambunctious, inventive words that were the common currency of Beat poetry in the fifties and Happenings in the sixties. He taught with Allan Kaprow, the creator of Happenings, at Rutgers in the late 1950s and early 1960s, who showed him that "art doesn't have to look like art."[1] A 1962 installation by Kaprow, entitled *Words,* was a room filled with such words as BLAM, THUNDER, SUCH MUSIC, THE MOCKERY, FUG IT, FOOL PROOF, JUNK, DON'T SQUEAL, and POW! WOW! These words became the roots of Lichtenstein's Pop consciousness. Long after he last placed a word in a cartoon bubble, he was using words in his interiors. And the words Lichtenstein chose show that over the years his art came to be more explicitly about the conception, reproduction, and viewing of art.

The relation between words and pictures in Lichtenstein's art is apparent in a page from a 1990s sketchbook (see p. 24), in which the artist jotted ideas for his paintings *Idea* (1993; see p. 81) and *Post Visual* (1993; see p. 25). Two columns of words — Post visual, Dangling Participle, CANTO, POST Modern Speak, ILLUSION, ADDRESS, ISSUES, bravura, dazzling, painting, concrete, male, thought, subject, object, concept, gender, idea, tour de force, FORM, content, End game, Issues, meaning — fill most of the page. On the left side of the page Lichtenstein sketched a yellow Baroque frame with the word IDEA in it, which could be considered art in its purest form. Roy was always concerned with archetypes, and was driven to capture the essential in things. At the bottom of the page is a larger sketch of interlocking geometric forms with the words FORM, CONTENT, ISSUES, and MEANING placed within the composition, an ironic diagram of the basic elements of painting. In *Post Visual* the most prominent painting within the painting is an ironic diagrammatic canvas similar to this drawing, an abstract composition with the words POST VISUAL.

In many ways, *Idea* encapsulates the Lichtenstein aesthetic: an abstracted depiction of a depiction (that is, a painting of a painting) of an abstraction ("idea"), self-referential and ironically distant. In Lichtenstein's painting *Art* (1962; private collection), the word ART fills a yellow field. It is painting as icon. I think Roy must have enjoyed the finality of it — the ultimate, self-signifying signboard. But it was a dead end. In a November 1963 *Artnews* interview, Roy declared that he was "anti-contemplative, anti-nuance, anti-getting-away-from-the-tyranny-of-the-rectangle, anti-movement-and-light, anti-mystery, anti-paint-quality, anti-Zen, and anti all of those brilliant ideas of the preceding movements which everyone understands so thoroughly."[2] The painting "Idea" within the painting *Idea* is, like the painting *Art,* both a sign and a symbol. The flat, yellow, Baroque frame with black outline in the painting is simultaneously the essence and the antithesis of Baroque art. With its complex play of illusion, color, and form, *Idea* shows that Lichtenstein remained to the end "anti-getting-away-from-the-tyranny-of-the-rectangle." His interiors stretched the other anti-qualities to their ironic breaking points. For him the canvas rectangle held limitless possibilities.

NOTES

1. Quoted in Joan Marter and Simon Anderson, eds., *Off Limits: Rutgers University and the Avant-Garde, 1957–1963,* exh. cat. (New Brunswick, N.J.: Rutgers University Press, 1999), p. 137.

2. Interview with Roy Lichtenstein in G. R. Swenson, "What Is Pop Art?" *Artnews* 62, no. 7 (November 1963), p. 25.

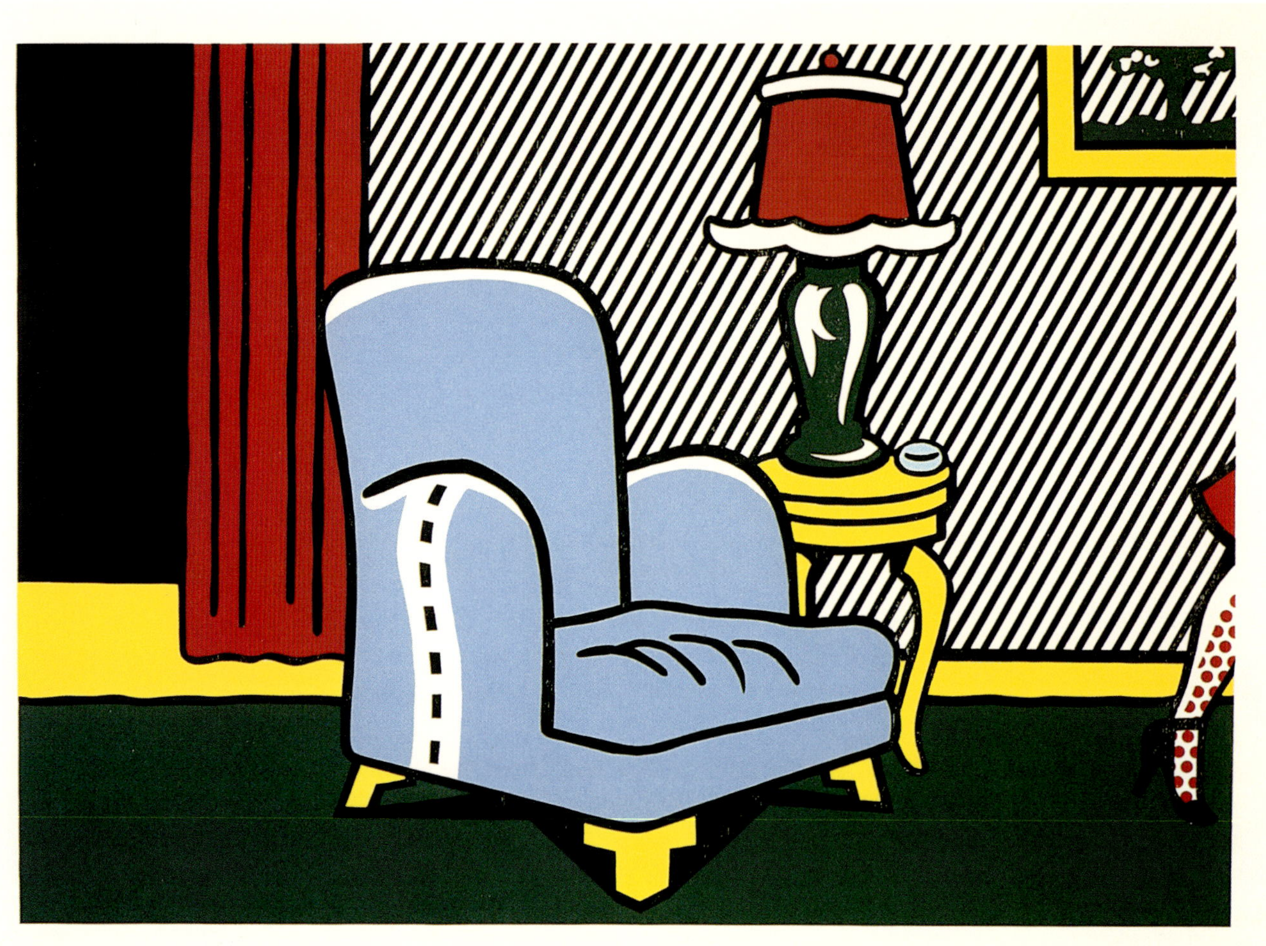

Roy

Sidney B. Felsen

Roy Lichtenstein made everything look amazingly easy. When I called him, he would likely be the one who answered the telephone. If I asked a question that needed looking into, he would invariably call back no later than the next day with a solution. If I set a date in April for Roy to

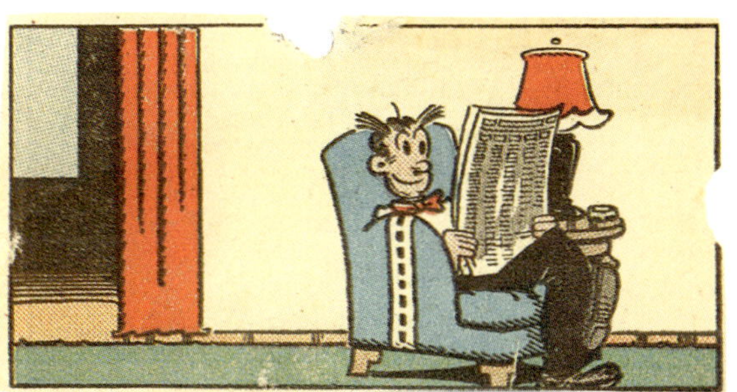

arrive at Gemini, the Los Angeles print workshop I co-own, on February 2 of the next year to stay six weeks, he'd be there as scheduled. He would arrive at the workshop each morning at nine o'clock prepared and ready for work. He worked a full day, setting goals for himself daily. Lunch was from one to three in the afternoon; it always began with a margarita, no salt.

And yet Roy was no automaton. There was a passion and a glowing interest in everything he did. I would say to myself: this is Roy Lichtenstein, not only a great artist but an industry, regularly producing extraordinary new bodies of work, supervising international exhibitions, and assisting in the completion of books and articles amidst the cacophony of several employees. This was one person, handling so much himself in a very personal way. How did he do it all?

One answer is that Roy worked all the time, whether it was at his art or his hobbies. Each year, there was one week at Christmastime when Roy and his wife, Dorothy, went to Captiva Island, in Florida. This was the extent of Roy's vacation time, but with it came a sketch pad so he would have something to do. I always thought Roy and Dorothy had a great relationship, but this is one area where they were miles apart. Dorothy was a constant, inquisitive traveler, often going to exotic places with friends, while Roy stayed home and made art or

Clipping from Lichtenstein scrapbook (*Blondie at Home Sweet Home*. Reprinted with special permission of King Features Syndicate).

LEFT
La Sortie (Gemini G.E.L. Interior Series), 1991. Cat no. 24.

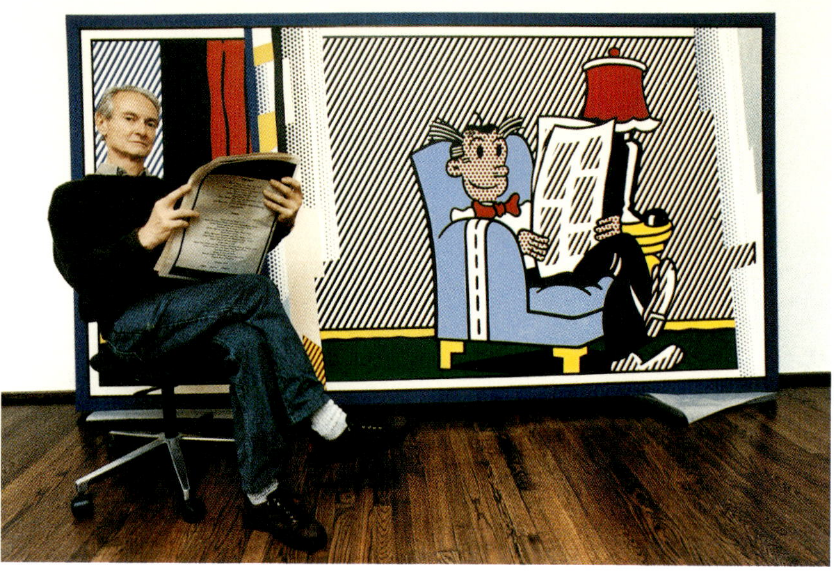

Roy Lichtenstein sitting in front of *Reflections: Sunday Morning* (1989; private collection, New York). Photograph © Bob Adelman.

RIGHT
Cathedral #5 and *Cathedral #6*, 1969. Lithographs; each 41 7/8 × 27 in. Gemini G.E.L., Los Angeles

explored his interest in music or science, about which he was an avid reader. In the later years of his life, Roy studied the saxophone seriously, taking lessons from Hayes Greenfield. One cool evening in Manhattan several of us accompanied him to the small Cyber Café where he played duets with his teacher. Roy kept repeating, "What am I doing here? I must be crazy." Nevertheless, we all thought he was actually very good.

I loved Roy's self-deprecating, ever-present, low-key sense of humor. Almost everything he said had a humorous twist or double meaning. This sense of humor, coupled with humility in spite of his fame, made him a candidate for many friendships. In my own observations, Roy's closest friendships were with Robert Rauschenberg and Ellsworth Kelly, and yet the friendships that Roy and Dorothy had with Irving Blum, Fred Tuten, Paul and Diane Waldman, and Jim and Kathy Goodman were probably the longest, and these remained active throughout his life. I was also well aware of his camaraderie with Jonathan Borofsky, Eric Fischl, David Hockney, Jasper Johns, Dorothea Rockburne, James Rosenquist, Julian Schnabel, and Richard Serra. During his later years, he developed strong friendships with Douglas Cramer and Michael Ovitz. As collectors, they appreciated Roy's work. There were many memorable moments, but one that says much about Roy was the evening when Michael and Judy Ovitz invited Roy and Dorothy to their home for dinner. They were invited as the special guests of honor, yet when they arrived they were amazed and overwhelmed to discover that their dinner companions were Kevin Costner, Tom Cruise, Dustin Hoffman, and Michael Eisner. As important as Roy was, he didn't ever expect the recognition he so deserved.

To no one's surprise but perhaps their own, Roy and Dorothy were on the A-list everywhere, but especially in New York, Los Angeles, and Southhampton. Together, they led a very active social life. Roy loved Dorothy very much and often commented, "I'm so boring — Dorothy adds the excitement to my life." I never thought Roy was boring, but Dorothy was definitely their social director. I do know that Roy was deeply involved in the lives of his sons, David and Mitchell.

David was a musician when I met him, and later began working in the computer industry while staying active with his music. Mitchell is an actor who has appeared both in movies and on the stage.

There was also a strong bond between Roy and his employees that was easy to feel when visiting the studio. He was concerned about them, and they were dedicated to him. Cassandra Lozano worked with Roy, and with Dorothy, for almost ten years; James de Pasquale for over twenty-five; Robert McKeever for almost fifteen; and Olivia Motch for ten. Carlos Ramos built Roy's sculpture maquettes for almost twenty-five years.

Roy's charity and loyalty within the art world were remarkable. Artists are constantly asked for contributions to innumerable organizations, be they political, medical, or social causes, and Roy was among the very few who always said yes. Moreover, we live in an era when very few artists stay with a gallery for a long period of time, and yet when I first met Roy in 1967 he was with the Leo Castelli Gallery, and he remained with Leo throughout his life.

And he was tremendously loyal to Gemini. In all, from 1968 through 1996, Roy made 124 editions at Gemini. For some reason, I presume it was because of the gloriously sunny days of Southern California, Roy always booked his Gemini proofing sessions for the month of February. He prepared in advance for each project, arriving with drawings or maquettes, or some form of studies. He had all the ideas well developed, with imagery, color choices, and scale established, yet he was open to the possiblity of changes that printmaking offers.

In his early works at Gemini, which include his *Cathedrals, Haystacks, Peace Through Chemistry, Modern Heads,* and *Bulls* series, the imagery was created by Roy and then transferred onto printing plates. In 1978 he made the decision to draw directly onto the printing elements. He asked for teaching and guidance from us, and we assigned Master Printer Ed Henderson to work with him. They spent a few days together in the artist's studio practicing with litho pencils and crayons, and out of the process developed the *Surrealist Series.* From that time, Roy used hand-drawing or carving in making virtually all of his prints. He used to say, "I want them to be hand-drawn but look mechanical."

Most of Roy's later Gemini projects, including the *Interiors Series,* were woodcuts. They started out being moderate in scale and eventually shifted to giant sizes; we twice enlarged our front litho press, ending up with a bed-size that is now 100 by 70 inches. For several weeks at a time, Roy would carve every day, always choosing to use a simple X-acto knife rather than any sophisticated power tools we offered him. He carved all the lines on the blocks, and we would

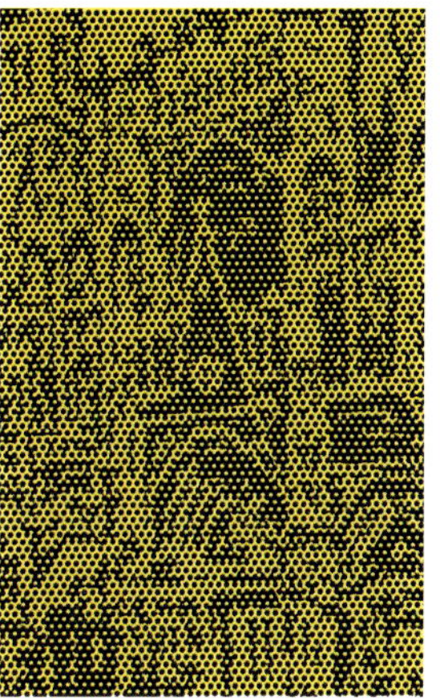

AUTHOR'S NOTE

I wish to express my deep gratitude to Joni Moisant Weyl for her assistance with this essay.

carve out the areas between the lines he established. Roy preferred Baltic birch plywood, as it was soft enough to carve yet tough enough to take the pressure from the press. Nevertheless, after days of carving, Roy's right hand would become noticeably red and sore.

At the same time as Roy explored hand-drawn or hand-carved printing elements, he began to use actual painted brushstrokes as well as a sponge to simulate plant life. He dedicated many hours in the artist's studio to practicing and developing these techniques for his printmaking. This is one of the several reasons why, throughout the years of collaborations, everyone at Gemini loved working with Roy. His commitment to printmaking combined with his easygoing style made it rewarding to give his projects the extra effort they often required. Roy had a great ability to talk to those of us in the workshop about his art eloquently yet simply, which I often thought came from his "pre-fame" years of teaching at the college level.

Before my partner, Stan Grinstein, and I started Gemini, I used to believe that artists who become famous rely upon their previous successes for the remainder of their lives. After being around Roy and his contemporaries, I realized quickly the folly of viewing them that way. These accomplished artists spend every hour of every day thinking about and working on their art. It's the only thing that really matters, other than their families. It's an obsession that grows stronger as they get older. This was an obsession that Roy clearly had.

Roy touched the lives of many people with his art. Those of us who knew him were also touched by his sense of humor, his honesty, his sense of fairness, his kindness.

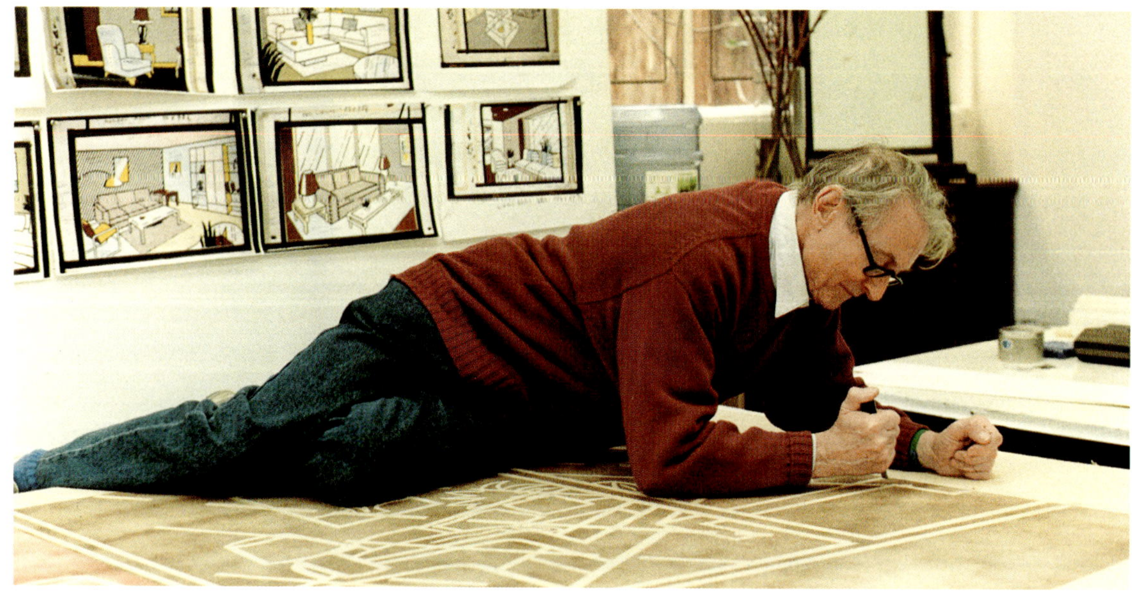

Roy Lichtenstein working on woodcuts at Gemini G.E.L., Februray 1990. Photograph © Sidney B. Felsen 1990.

Plates

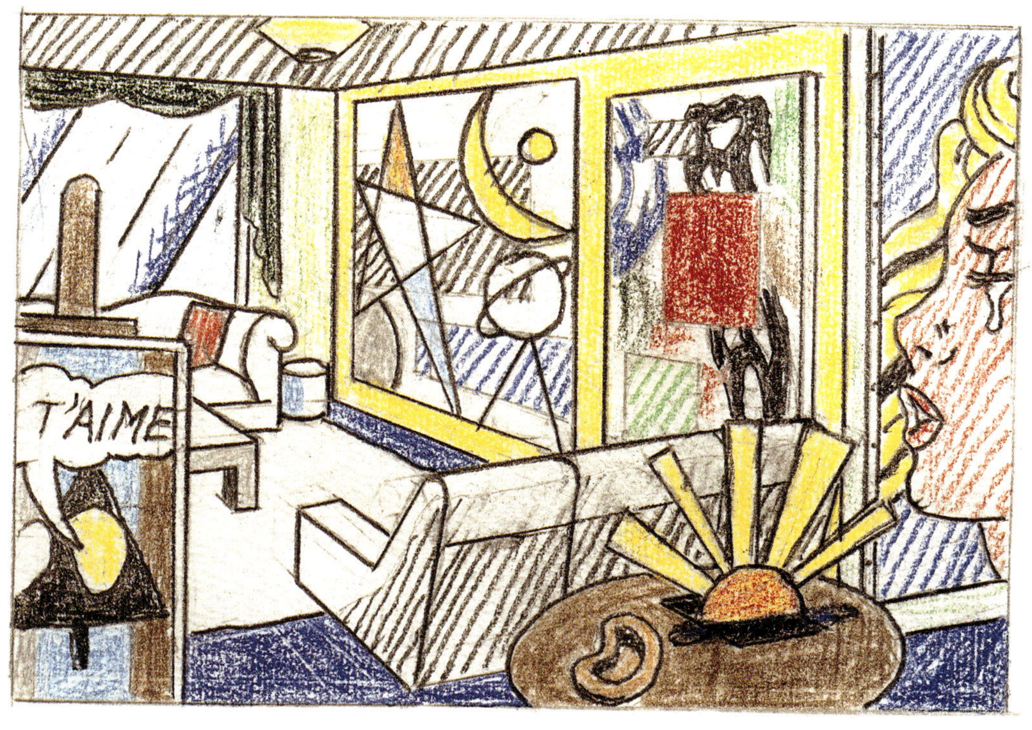

Interior with T'aime
(drawing for painting),
1993. Cat. no. 39.

Interior with T'aime, 1994.
Cat. no. 44.

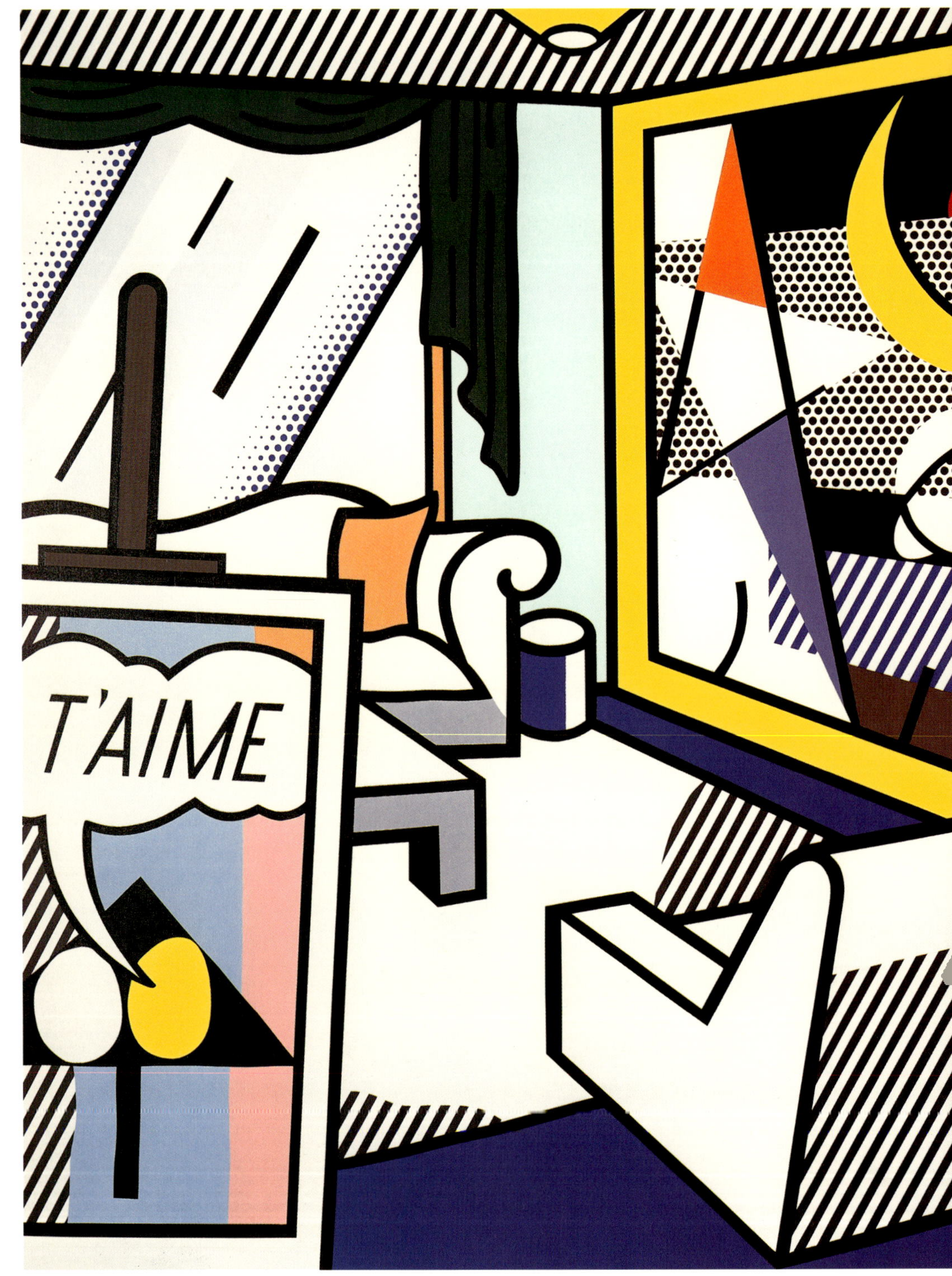

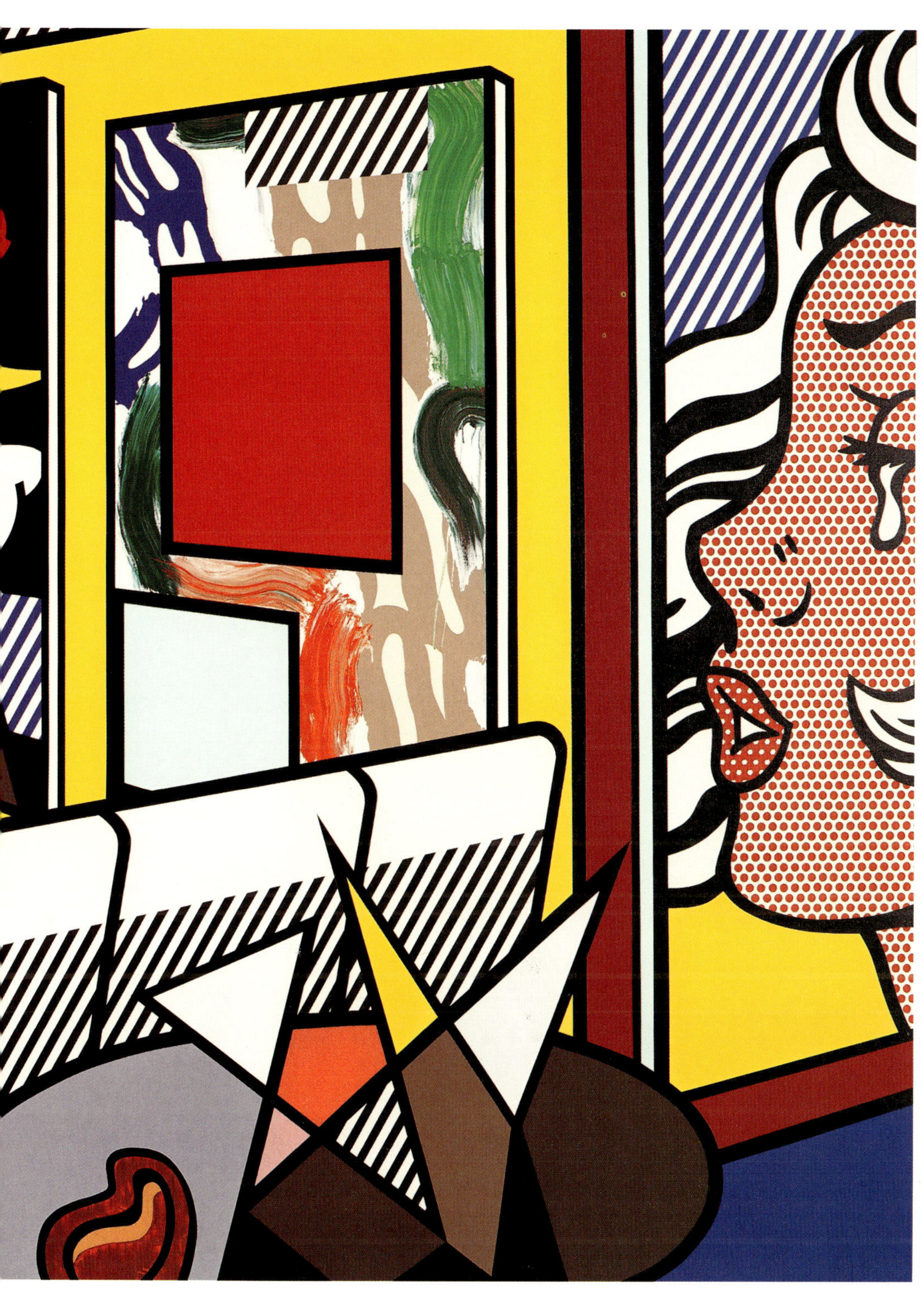

1 Robert Motherwell. *Je t'aime IV*, 1955–57. Oil on canvas; 70 1/8 x 100 in. © Dedalus Foundation, Inc. Licensed by VAGA, New York.

2 Details from sketches for *Interior with T'aime*, 1993. Cat. no. 42.

3 Clipping from Lichtenstein scrapbook.

4 ***Imperfect Sculpture***, 1995. Cat. no. 52.

RIGHT
Interior with T'aime (collage for painting), 1993. Cat. no. 38.

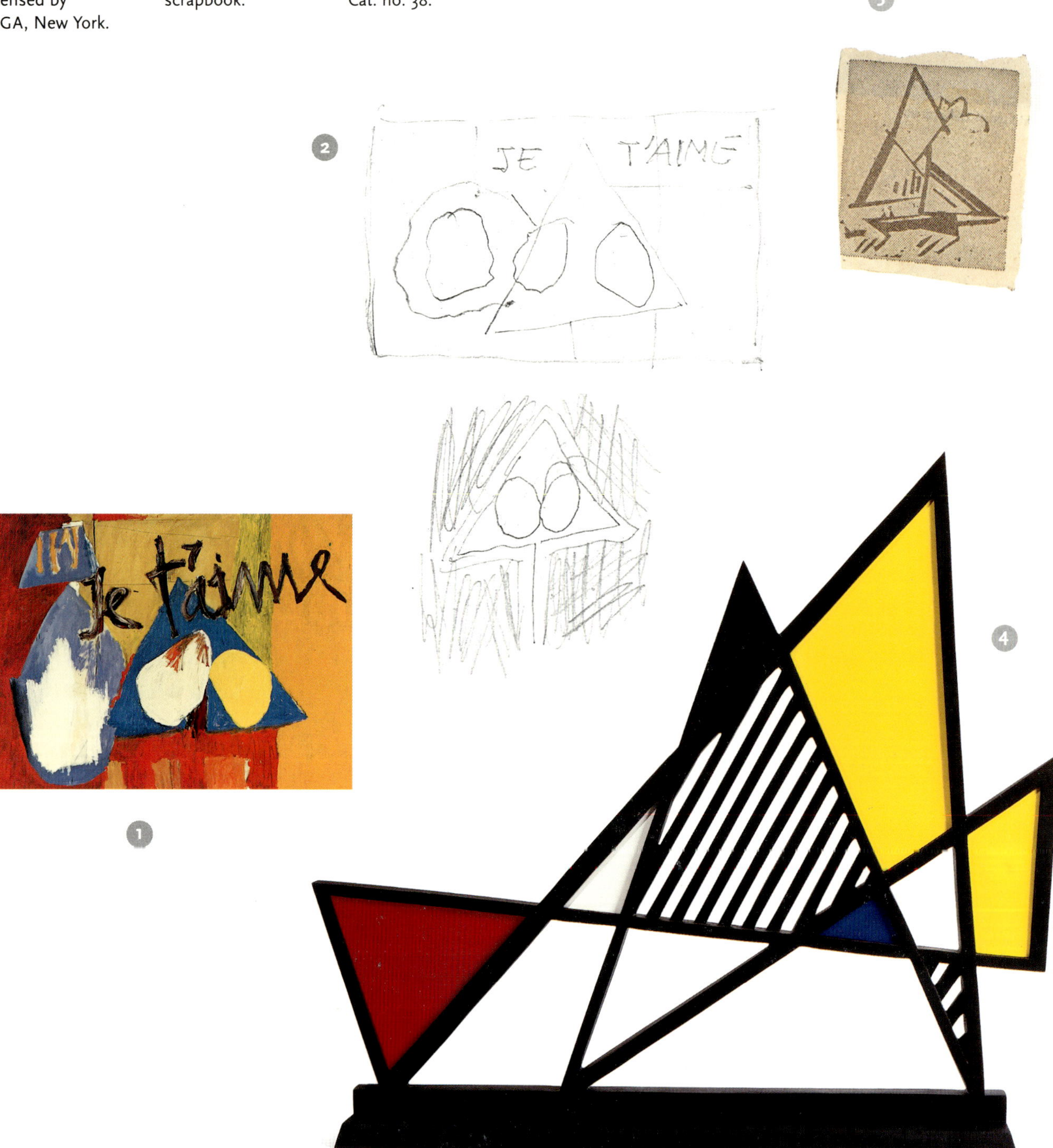

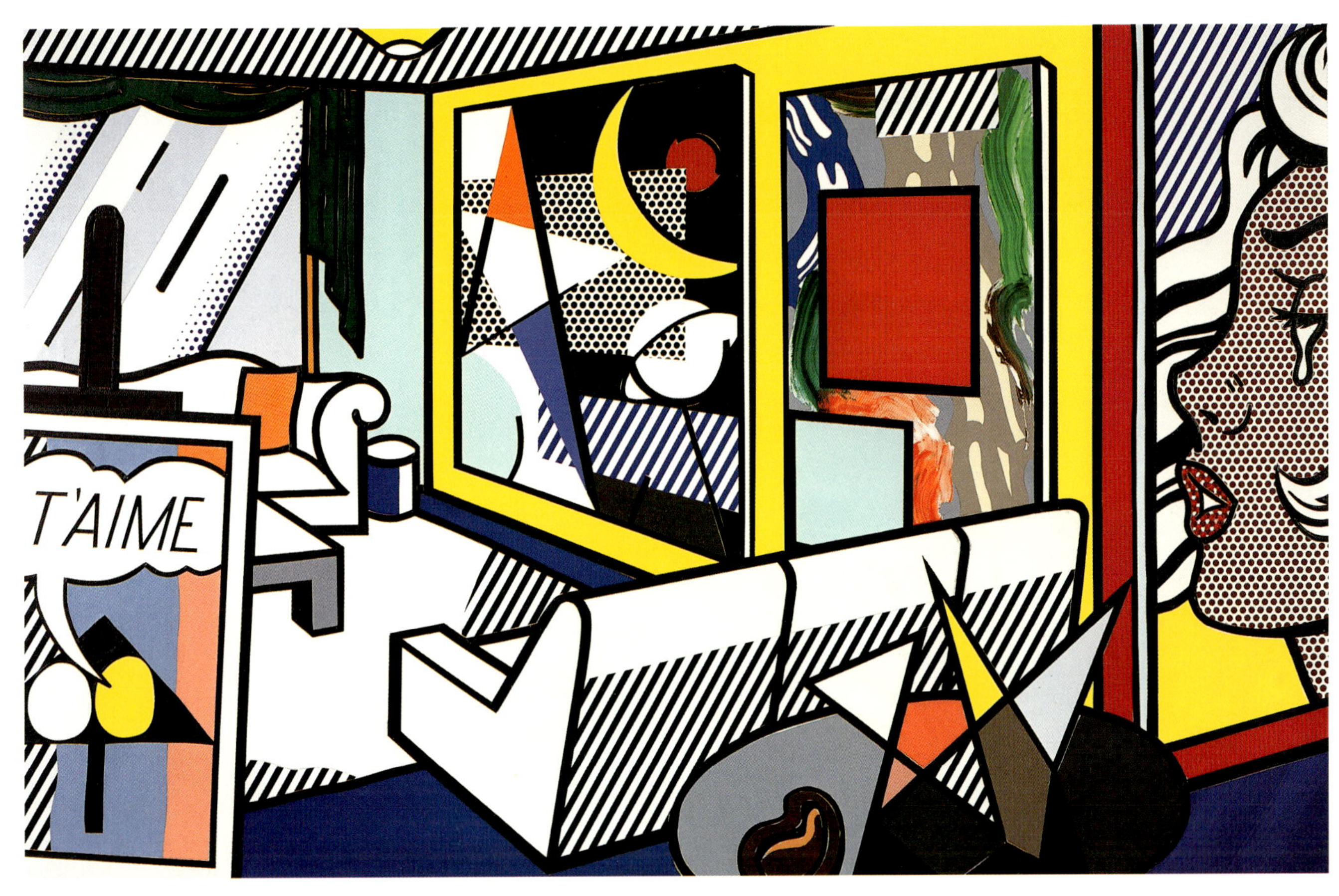
T'AIME

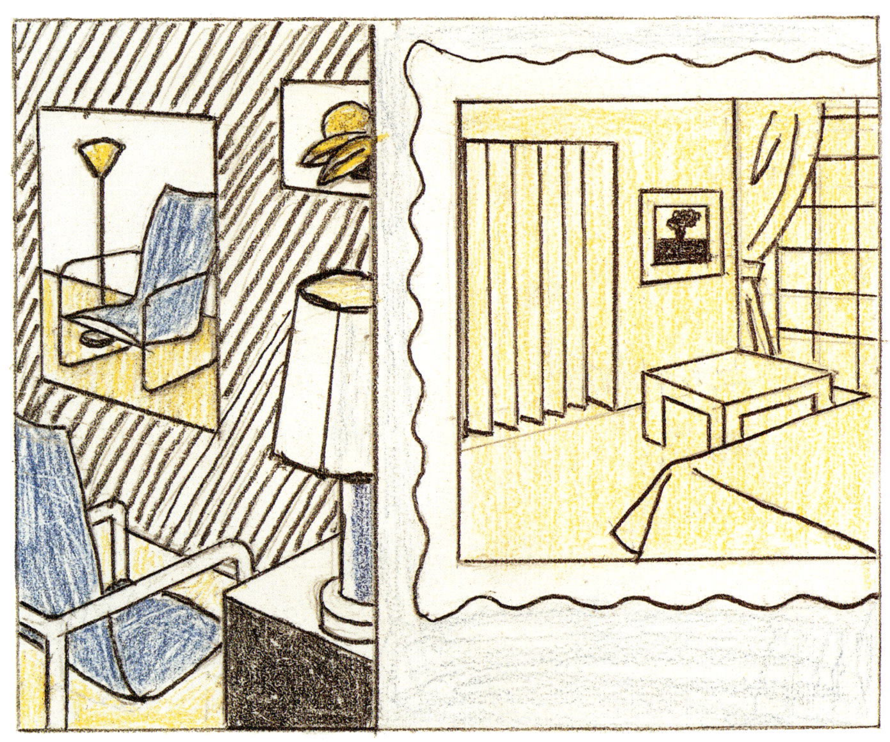

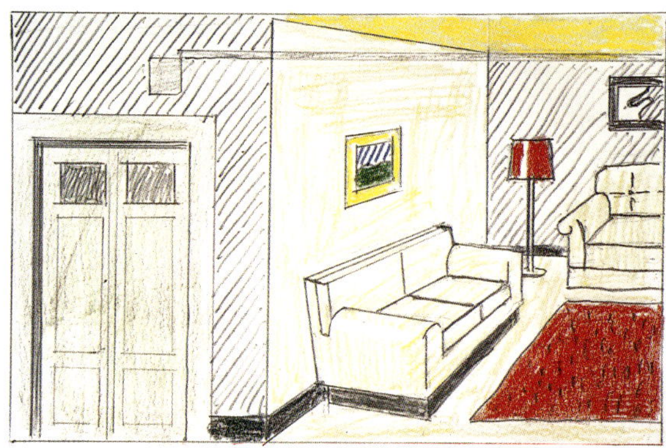

Interior with Motel Room Painting (drawing for painting), 1992. Cat. no. 30.

Untitled (drawing), 1989. Cat. no. 10.

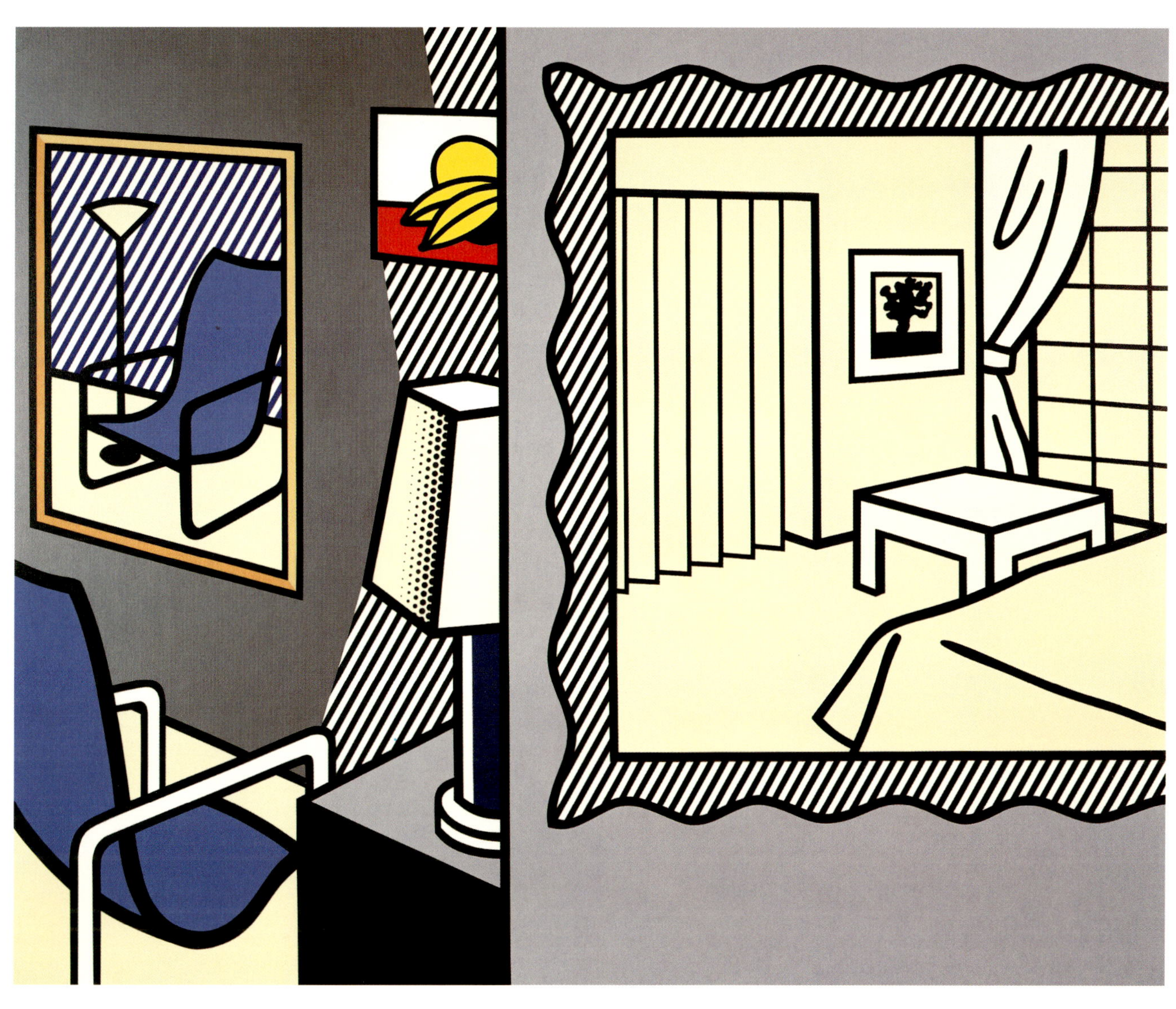

Interior with Motel Room Painting, 1992.
Cat. no. 29.

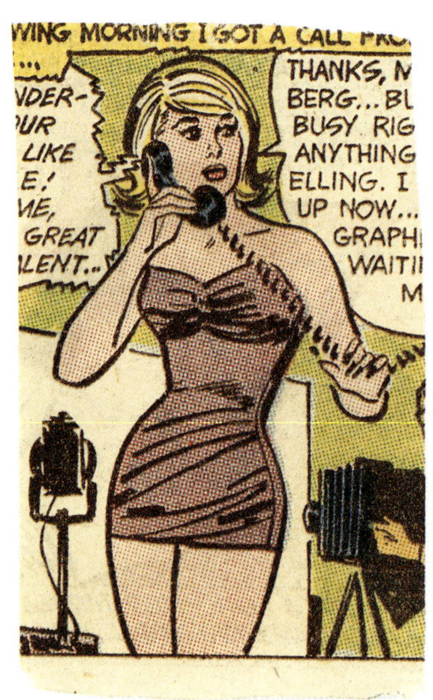

Clipping from Lichtenstein scrapbook (*Girls' Love Stories*, no. 97 © 1963 DC Comics).

RIGHT
Nude with Yellow Flower, 1994.
Cat. no. 48.

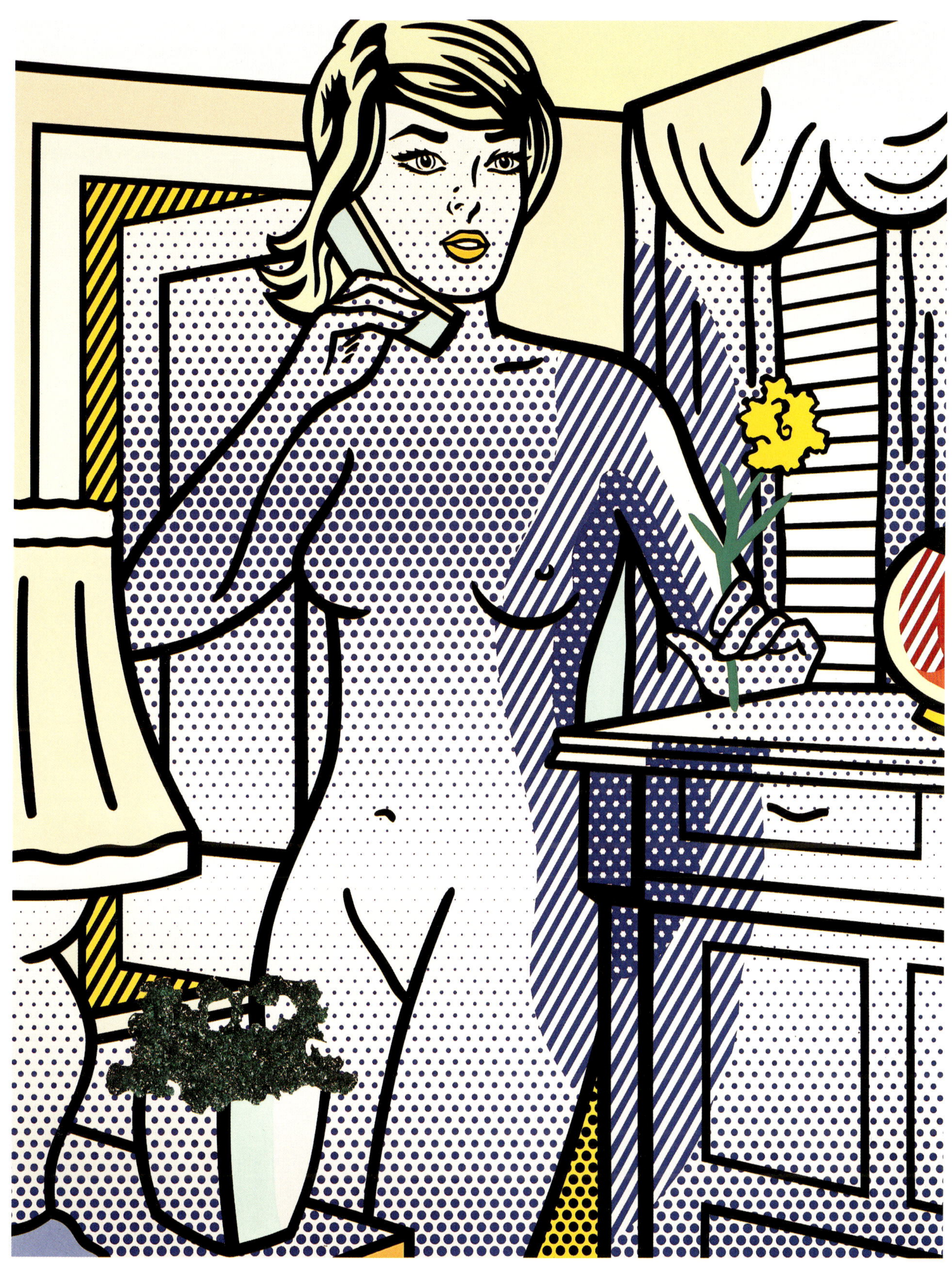

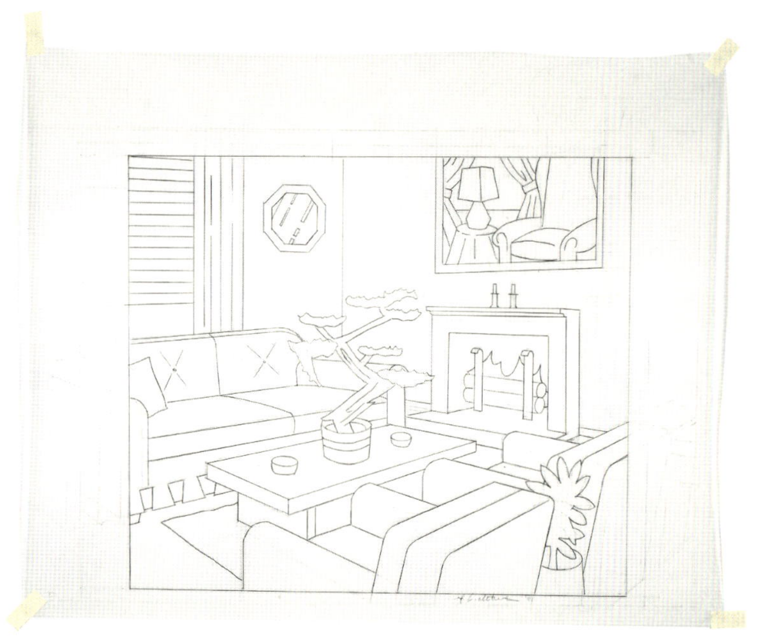

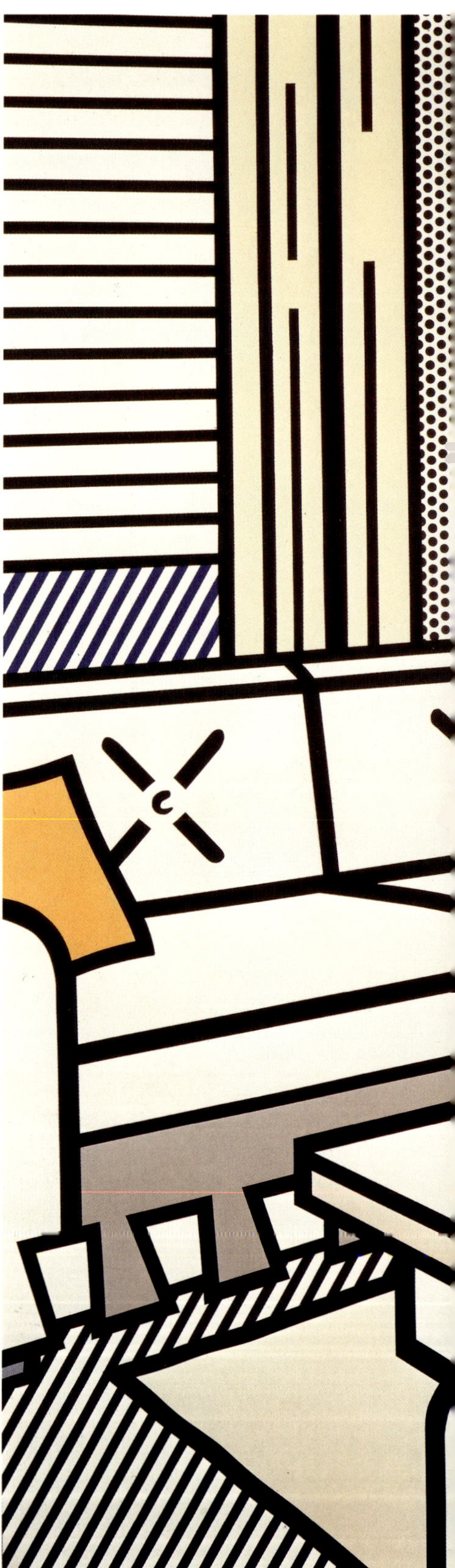

Interior with Bonsai Tree
(drawing for painting),
1991. Cat. no. 17.

Interior with Bonsai Tree,
1991. Cat. no. 16.

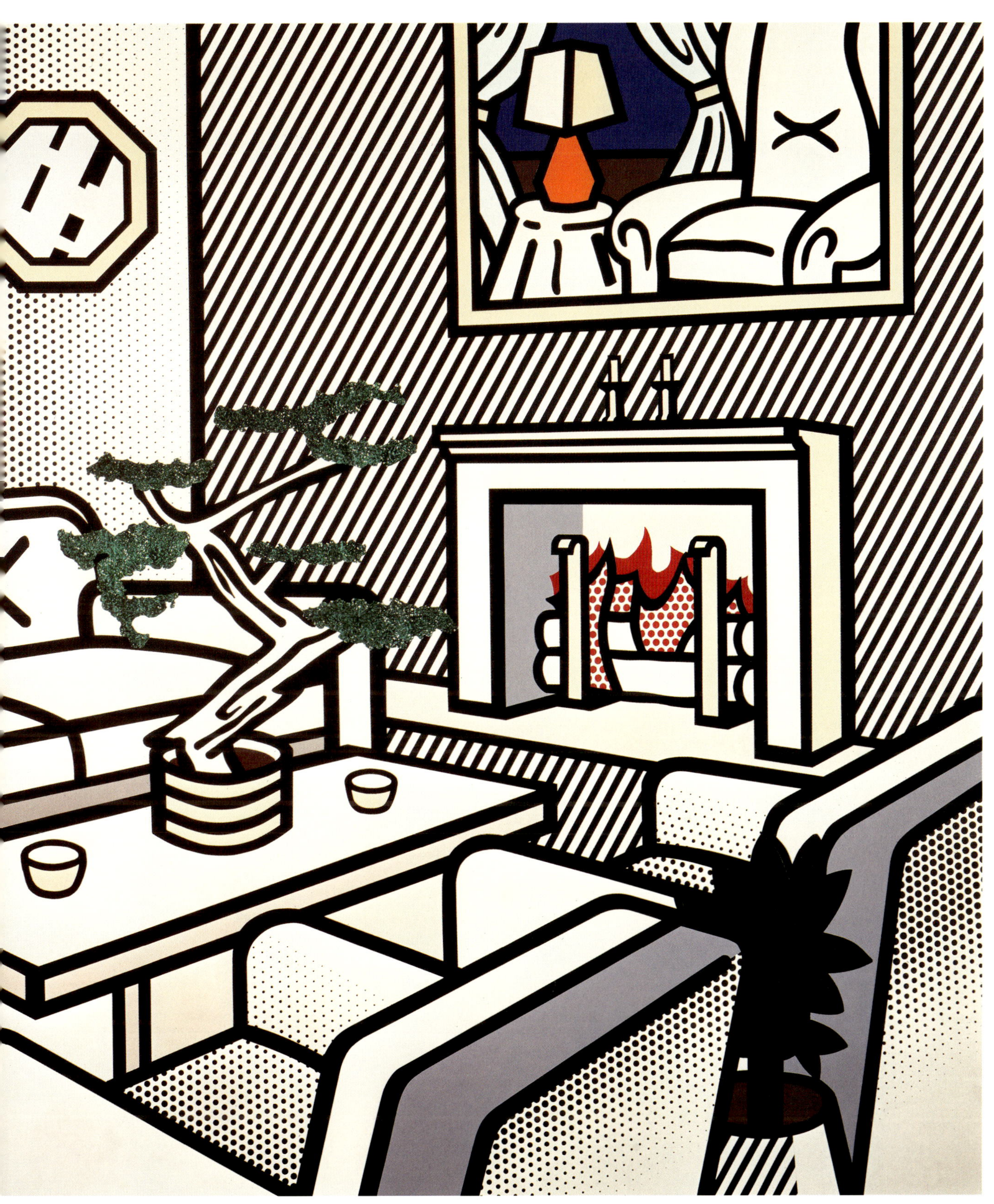

1 ***Bonsai Tree***, 1992. Cat. no. 26.

2 ***Bonsai Tree*** (drawing for sculpture), 1992. Cat. no. 27.

3 Clipping from Lichtenstein scrapbook.

4 Clipping from Lichtenstein scrapbook.

RIGHT
Interior with Bonsai Tree (detail), 1991. Cat. no. 16.

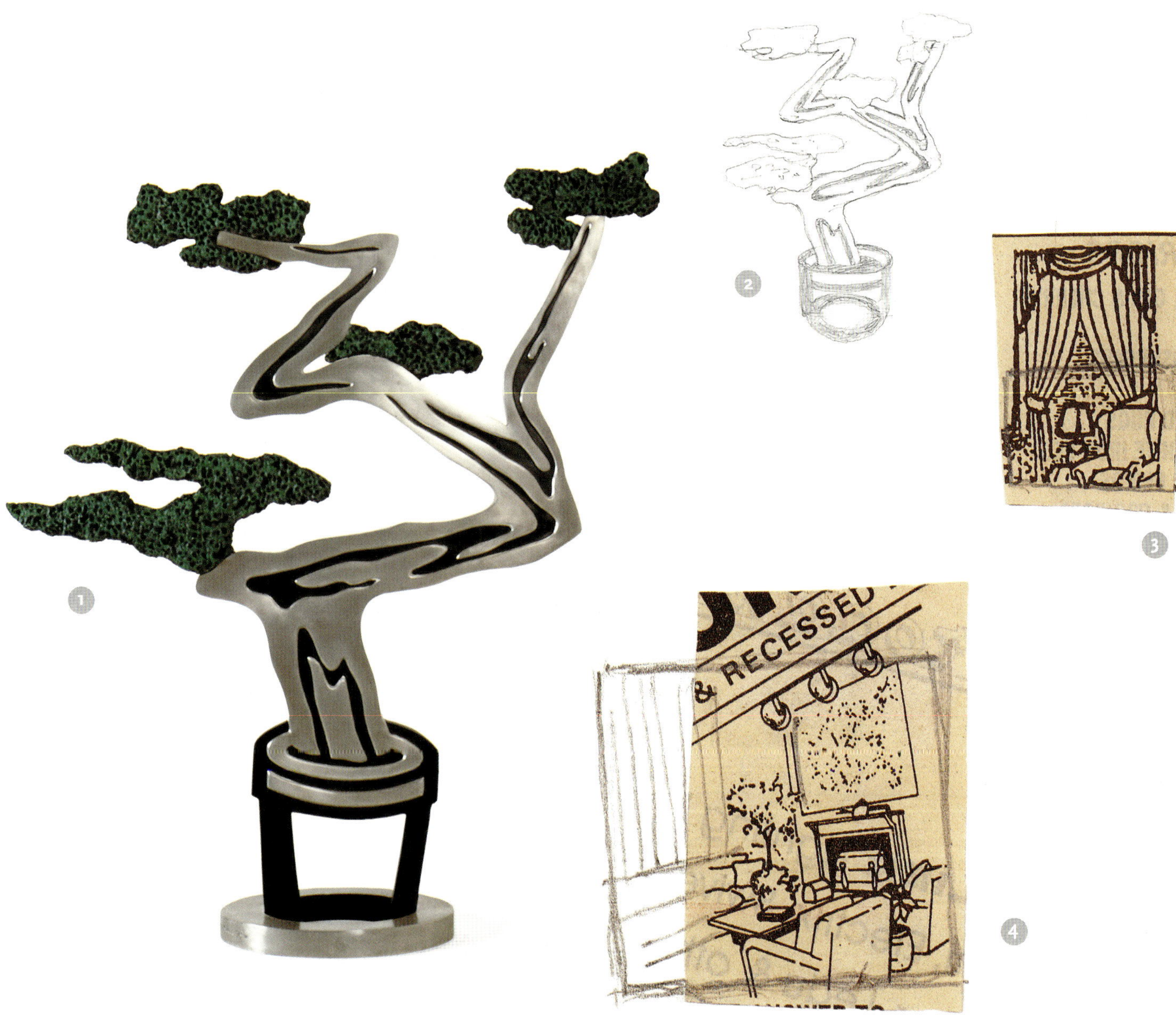

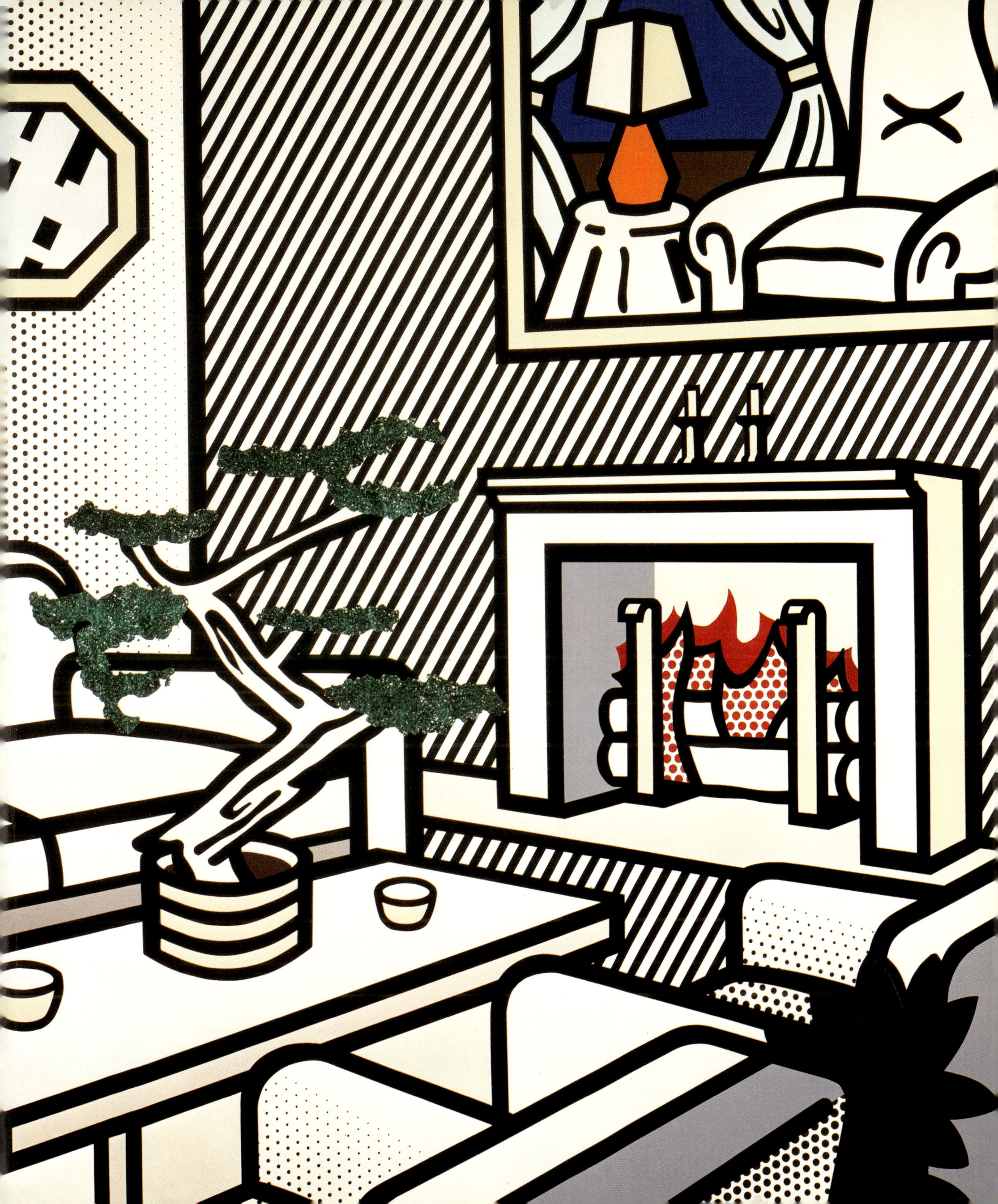

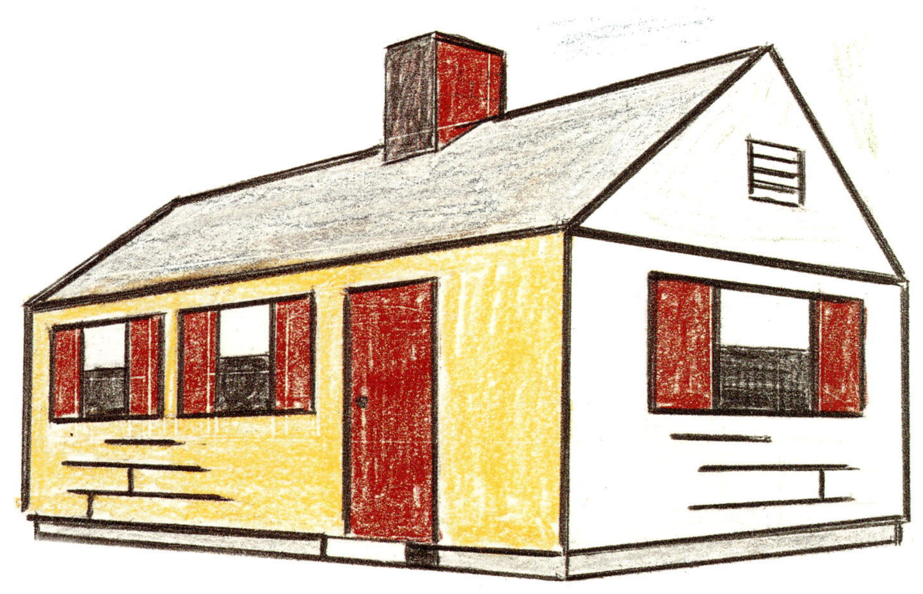

House with
Gray Roof, 1997.
Cat. no. 61.

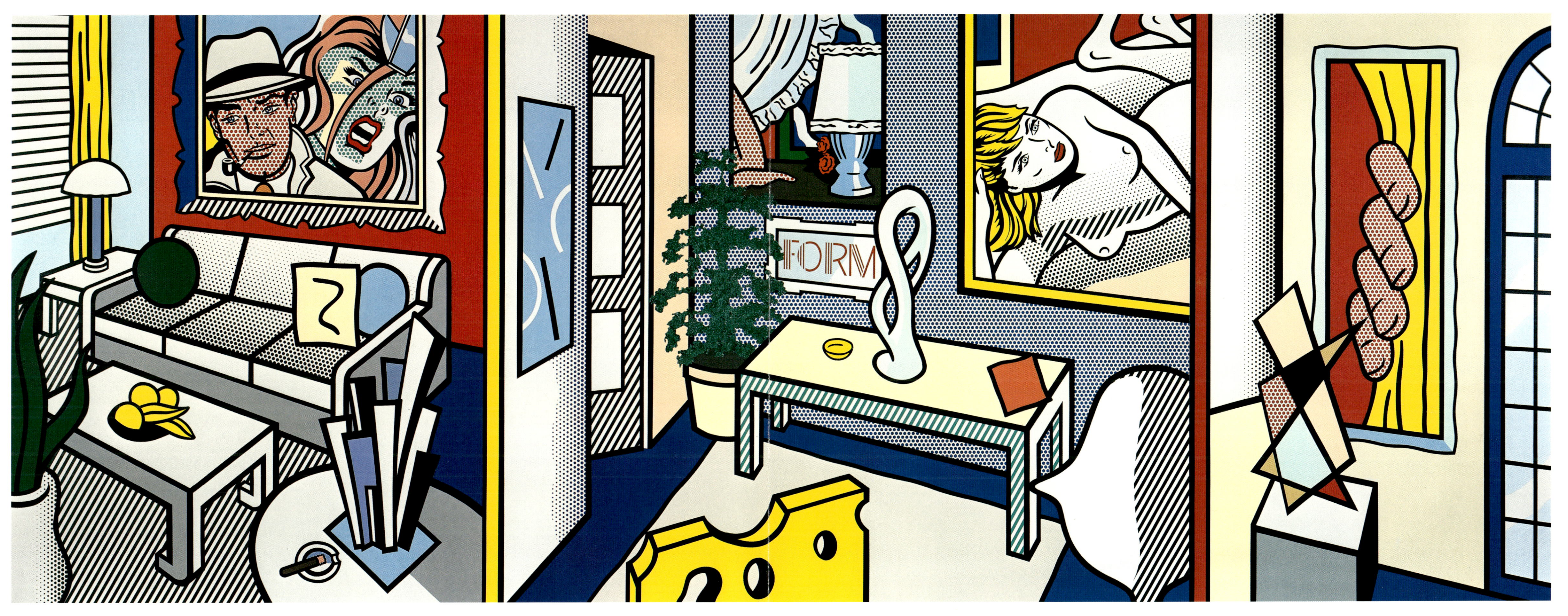
FORM

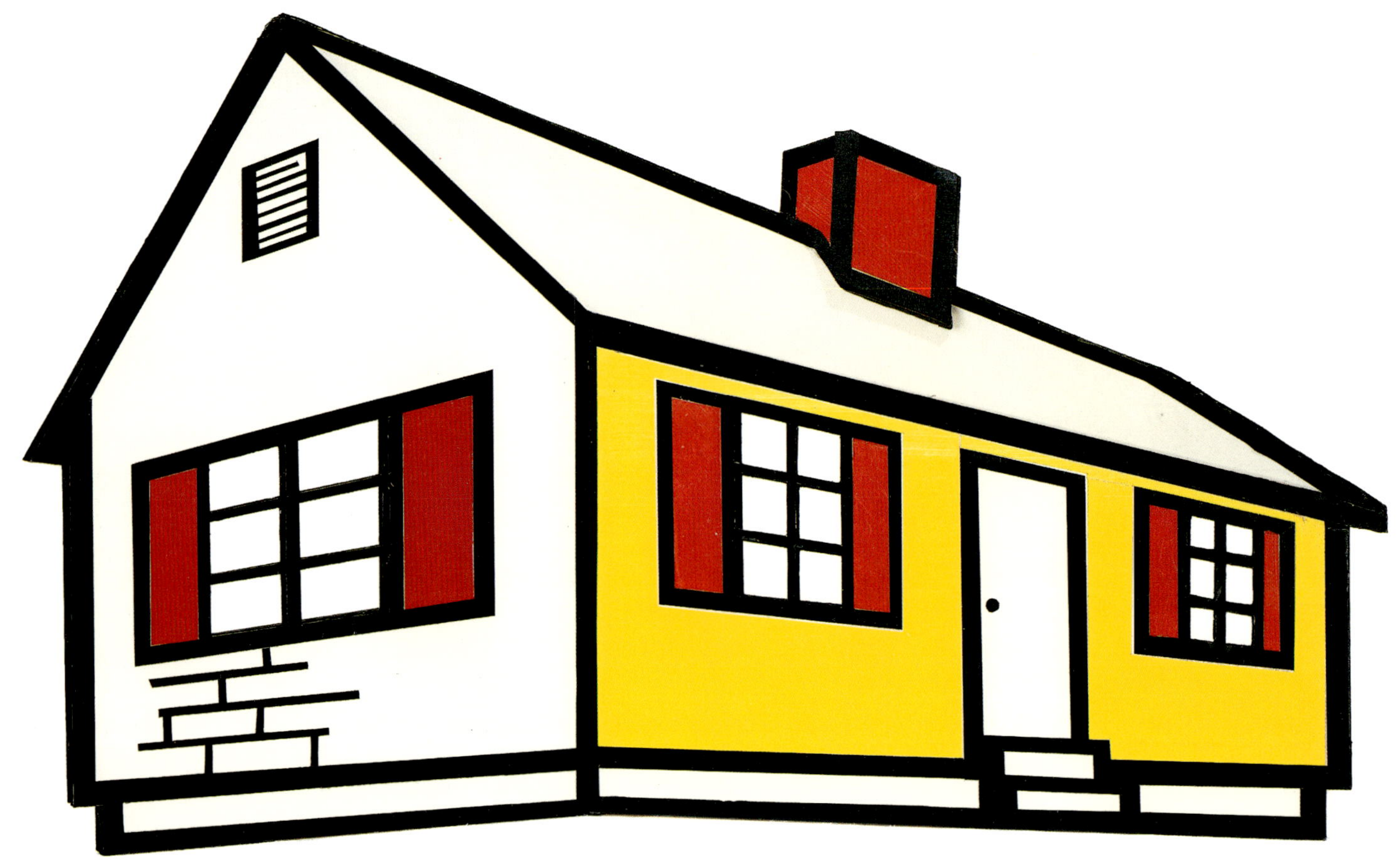

House I (maquette
for sculpture), 1997.
Cat. no. 60.

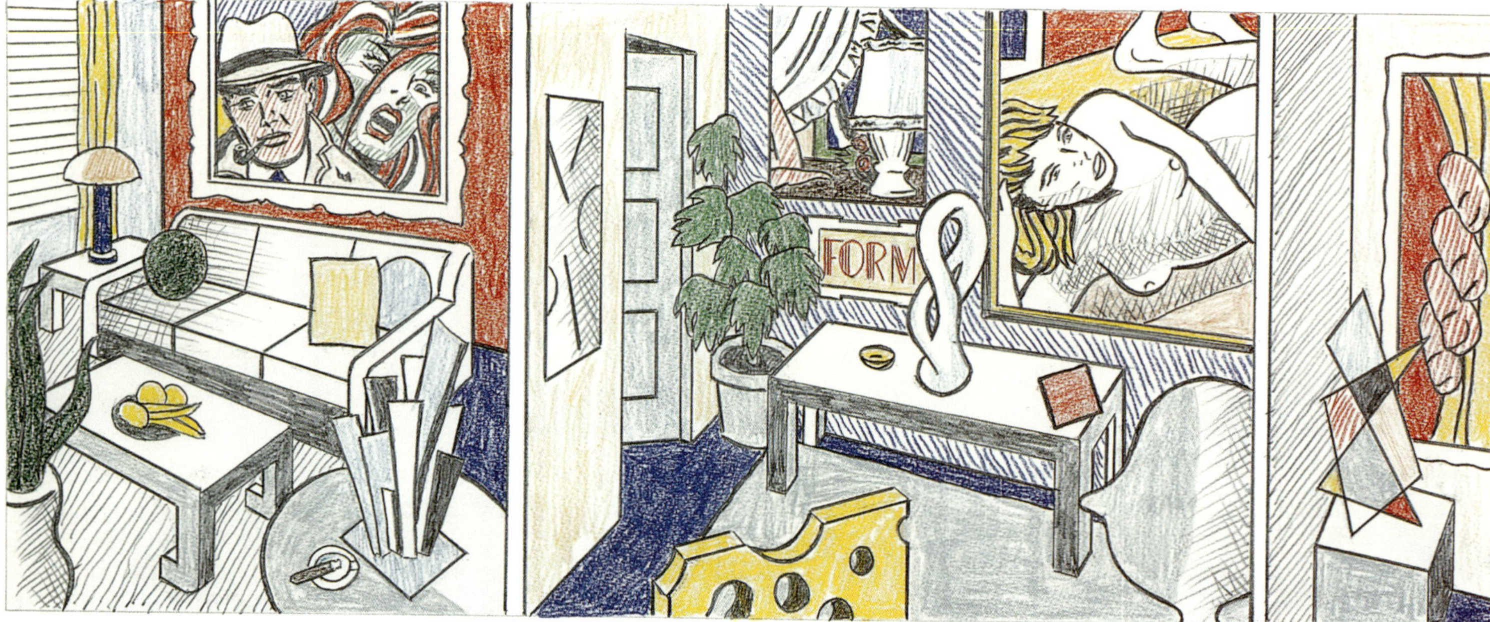

***Large Interior with
Three Reflections***
(drawings for painting),
1993. Cat. no. 41.

OVERLEA
***Large Int
Three Re***
Cat. no.

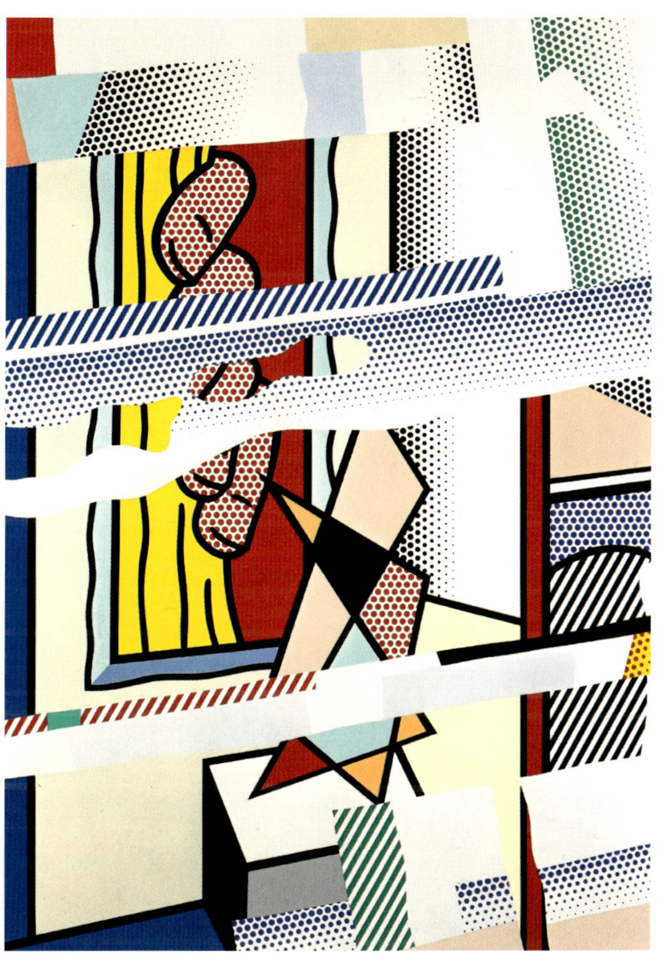

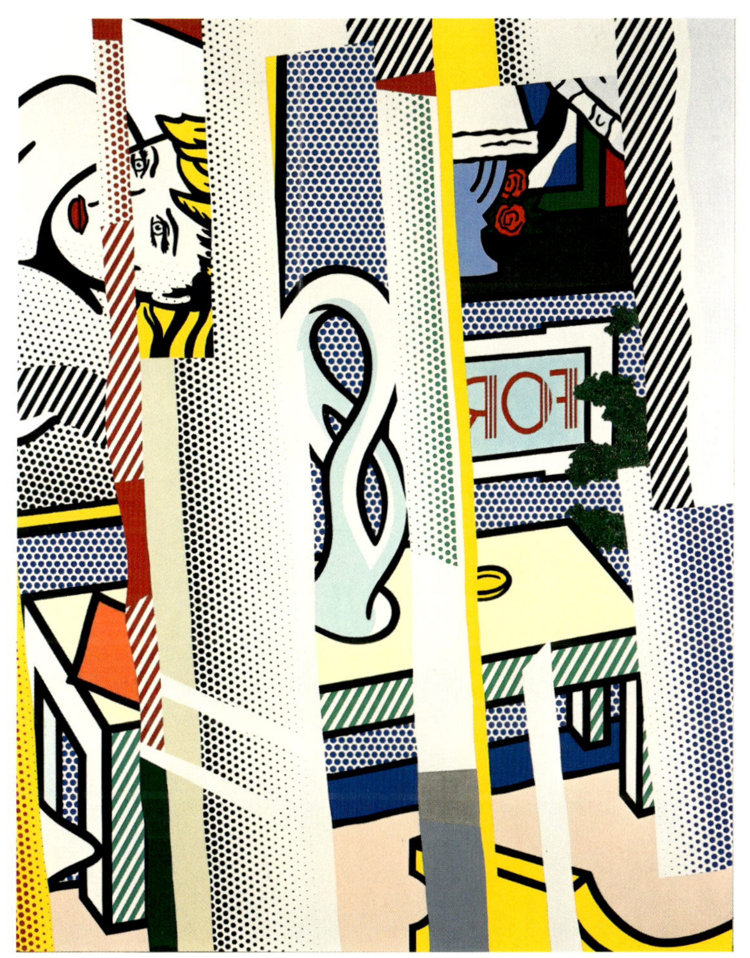

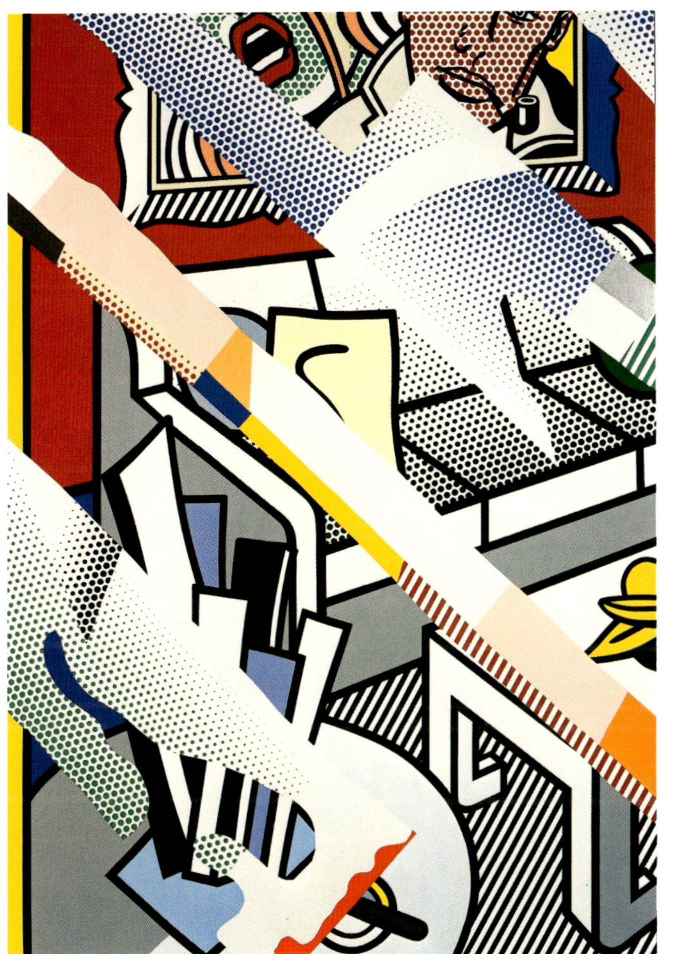

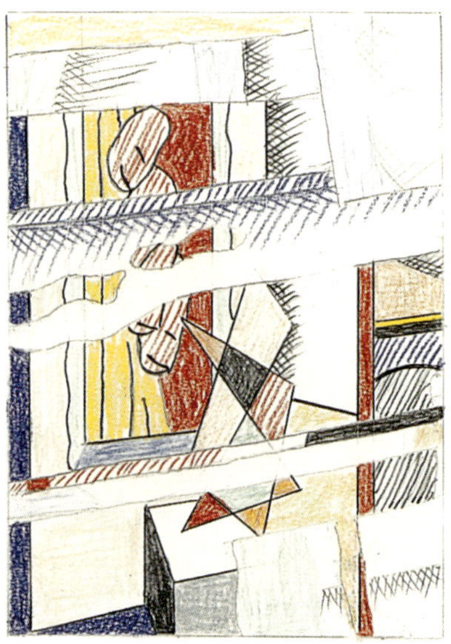

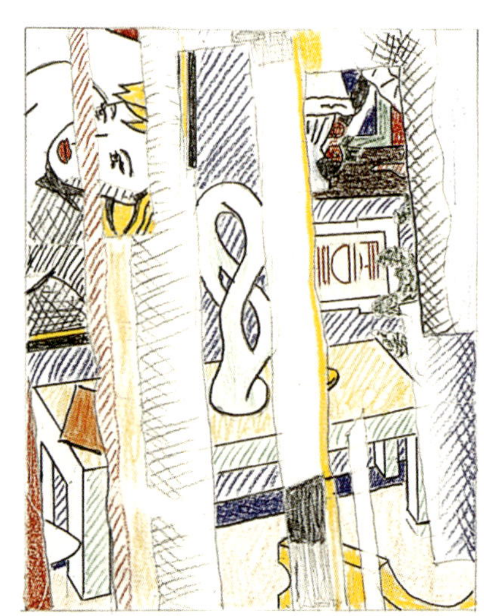

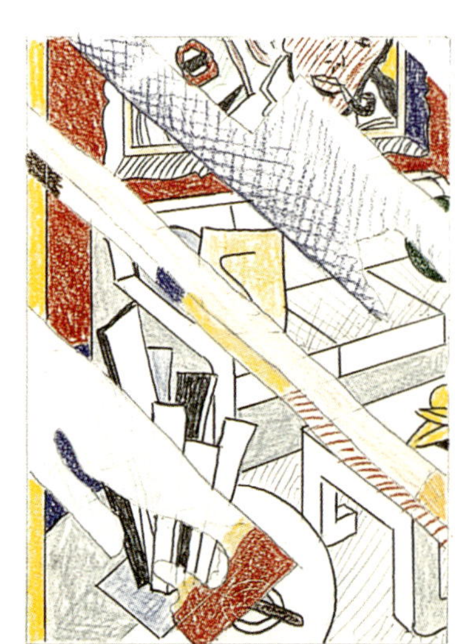

1 Clipping from Lichtenstein scrapbook.

2 ***Bananas and Grapefruit I***, 1972. Cat. no. 4.

3 ***Cityscape***, 1995. Cat. no. 50.

4 Clipping from Lichtenstein scrapbook (*Web of Spider-man*, vol. 1, no. 98, March 1993 © Marvel Characters, Inc.).

5 Details from sketches for *Cityscape*, 1993. Cat. no. 41.

6 Clipping from Lichtenstein scrapbook (*Secret Hearts*, no. 95, April 1964 © 1999 DC Comics).

7 Clipping from Lichtenstein scrapbook (*The Avengers*, vol. 1, no. 358, January 1993 © Marvel Characters, Inc.).

8 ***Large Interior with Three Reflections*** (sketch for painting), 1993. Cat. no. 43.

RIGHT
Large Interior with Three Reflections (detail), 1993. Cat. no. 40.

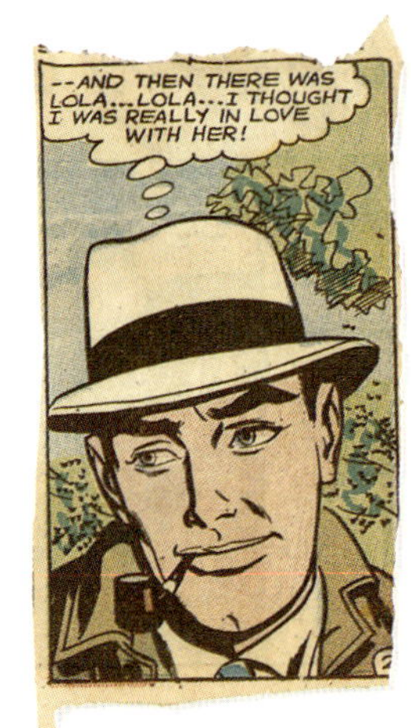

6

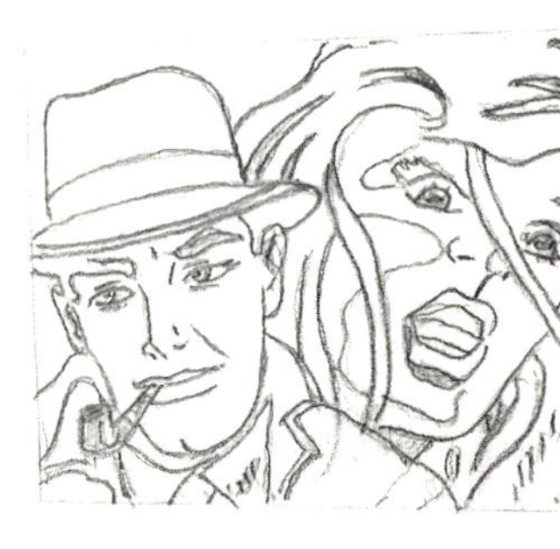

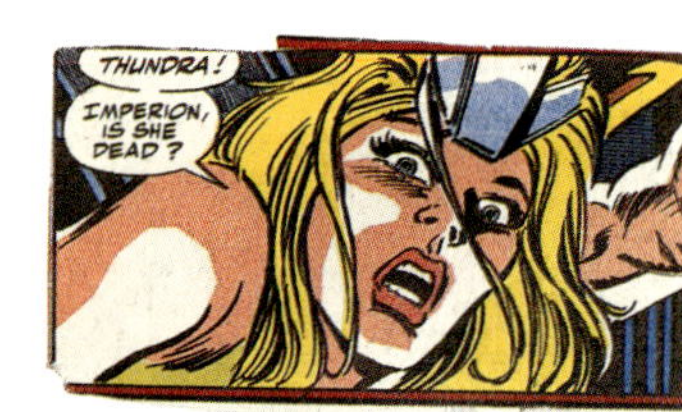

7

1

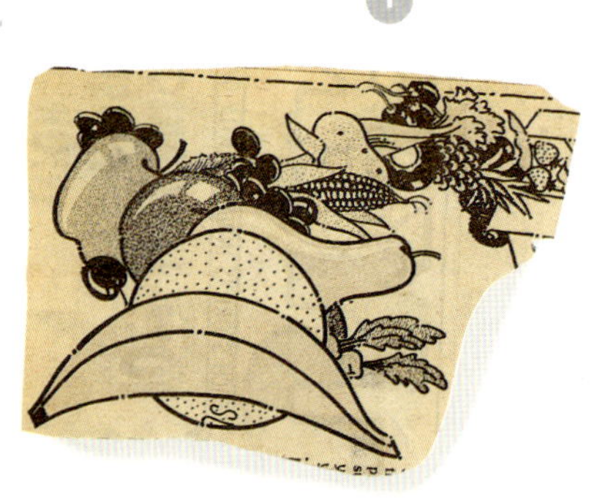

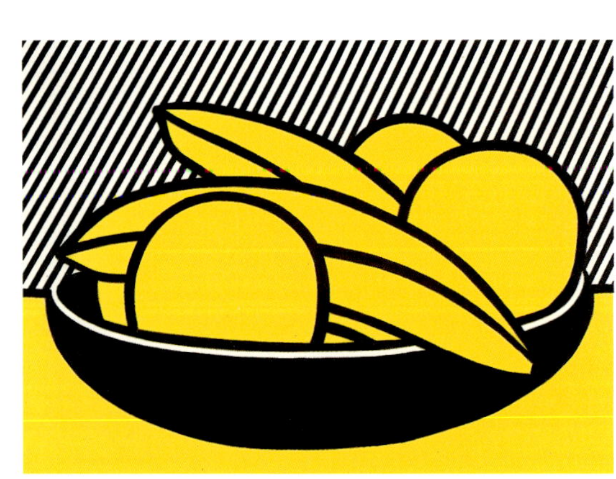

2

5

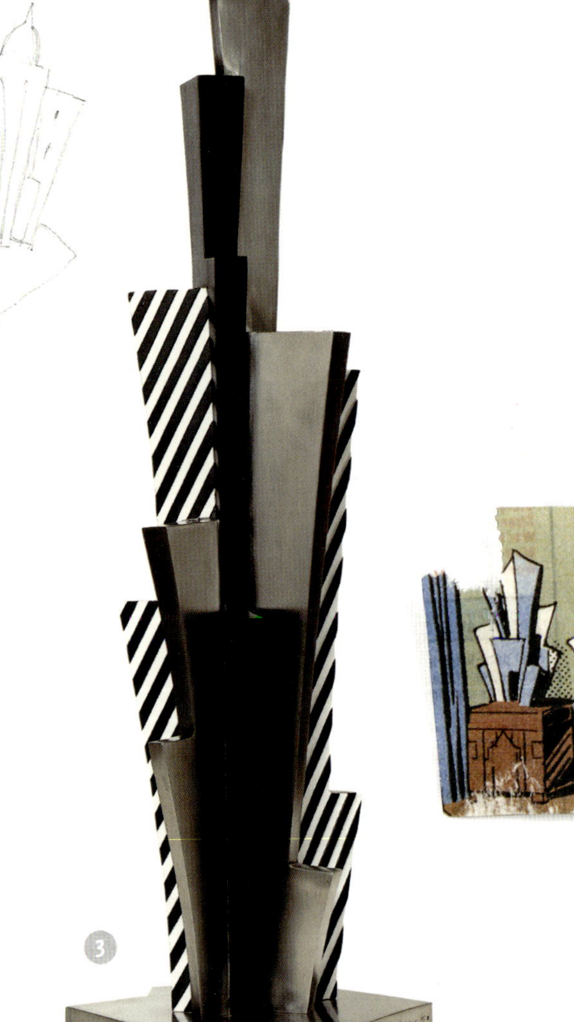

3

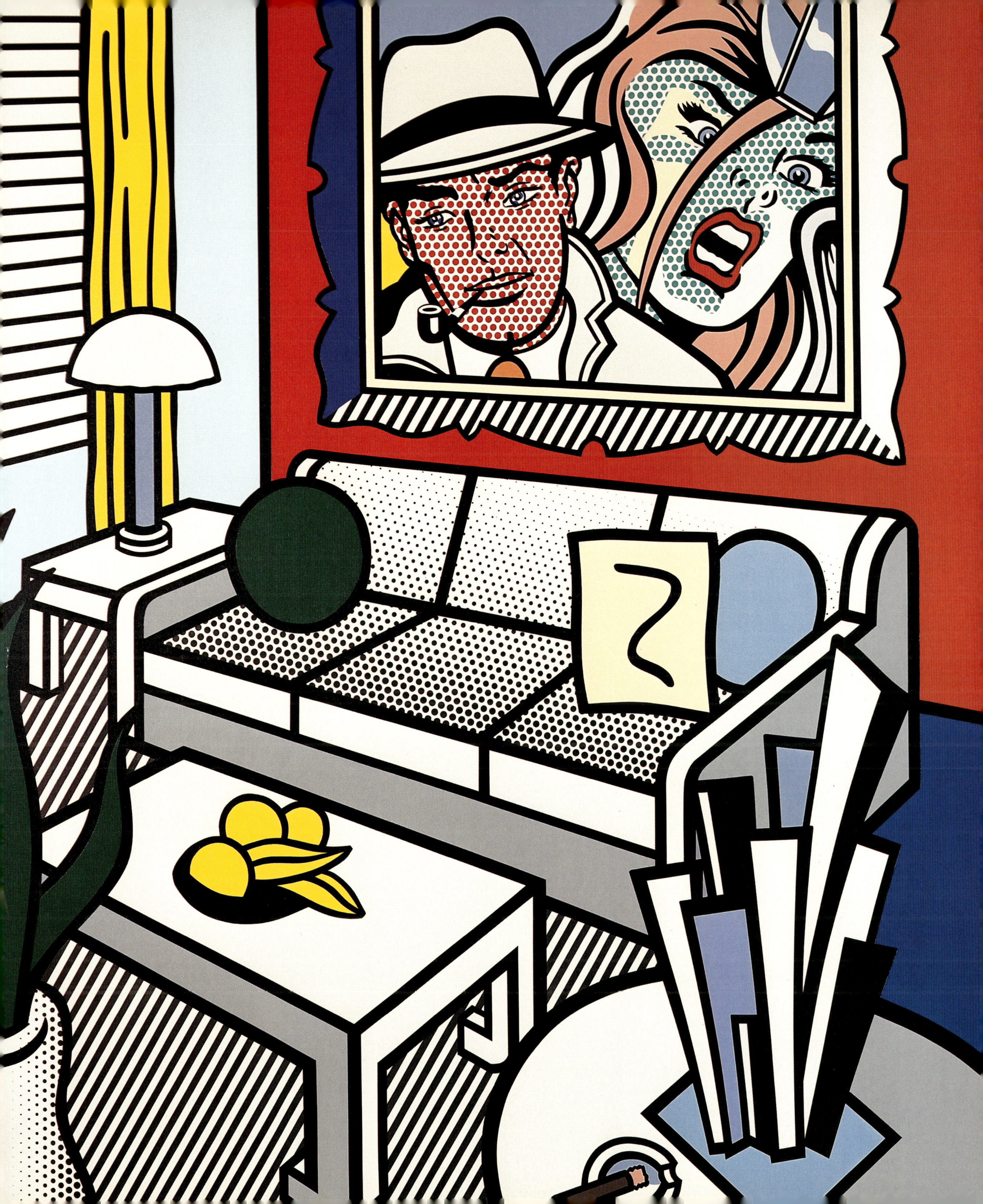

1 Clipping from Lichtenstein scrapbook (*Heart Throbs,* no. 78 © 1962 DC Comics).

2 *Swiss Cheese,* 1962. Oil on canvas; 40 × 40 in. David Lichtenstein Collection, New York.

3 Clipping from Lichtenstein scrapbook (*Tintin and the Picaros* © Hergé/ Moulinsart 1999).

4 Clipping from Lichtenstein scrapbook (*Young Love,* no. 40 © 1963 DC Comics).

RIGHT
Large Interior with Three Reflections (detail), 1993. Cat. no. 40.

4

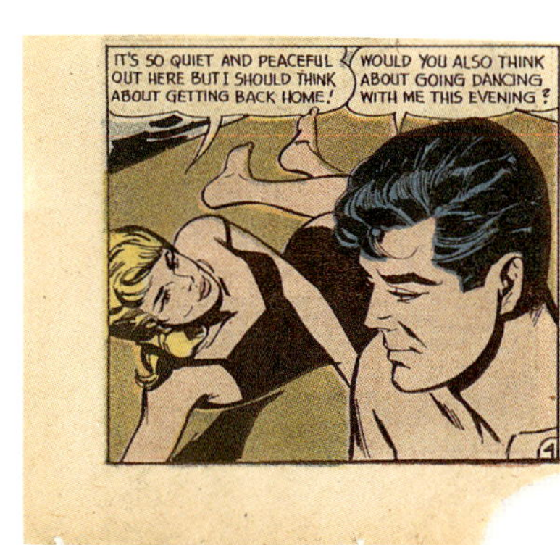

1

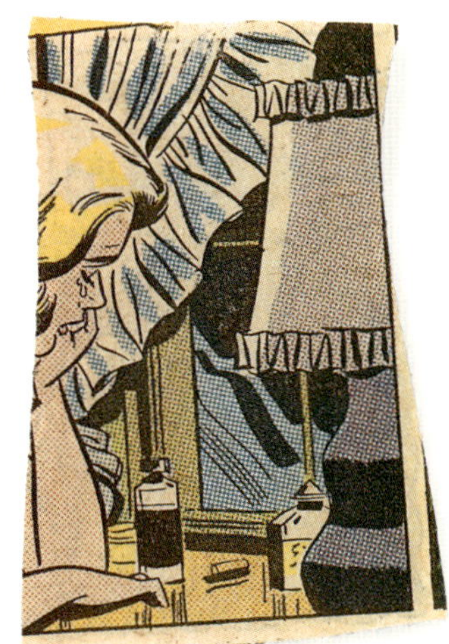

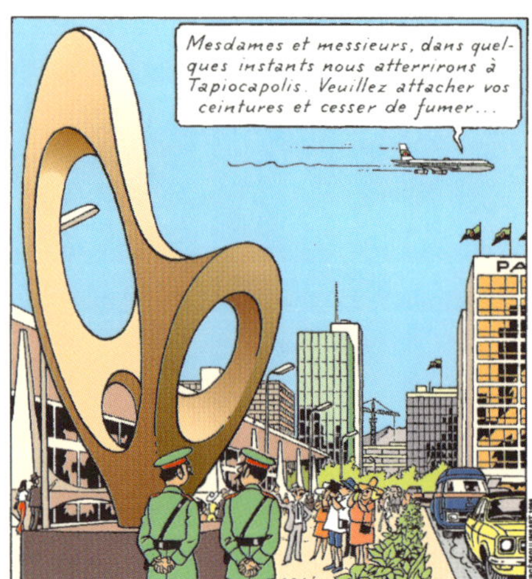

3

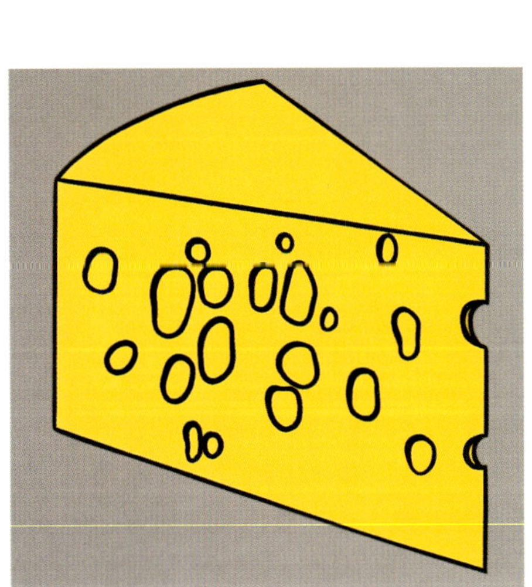

2

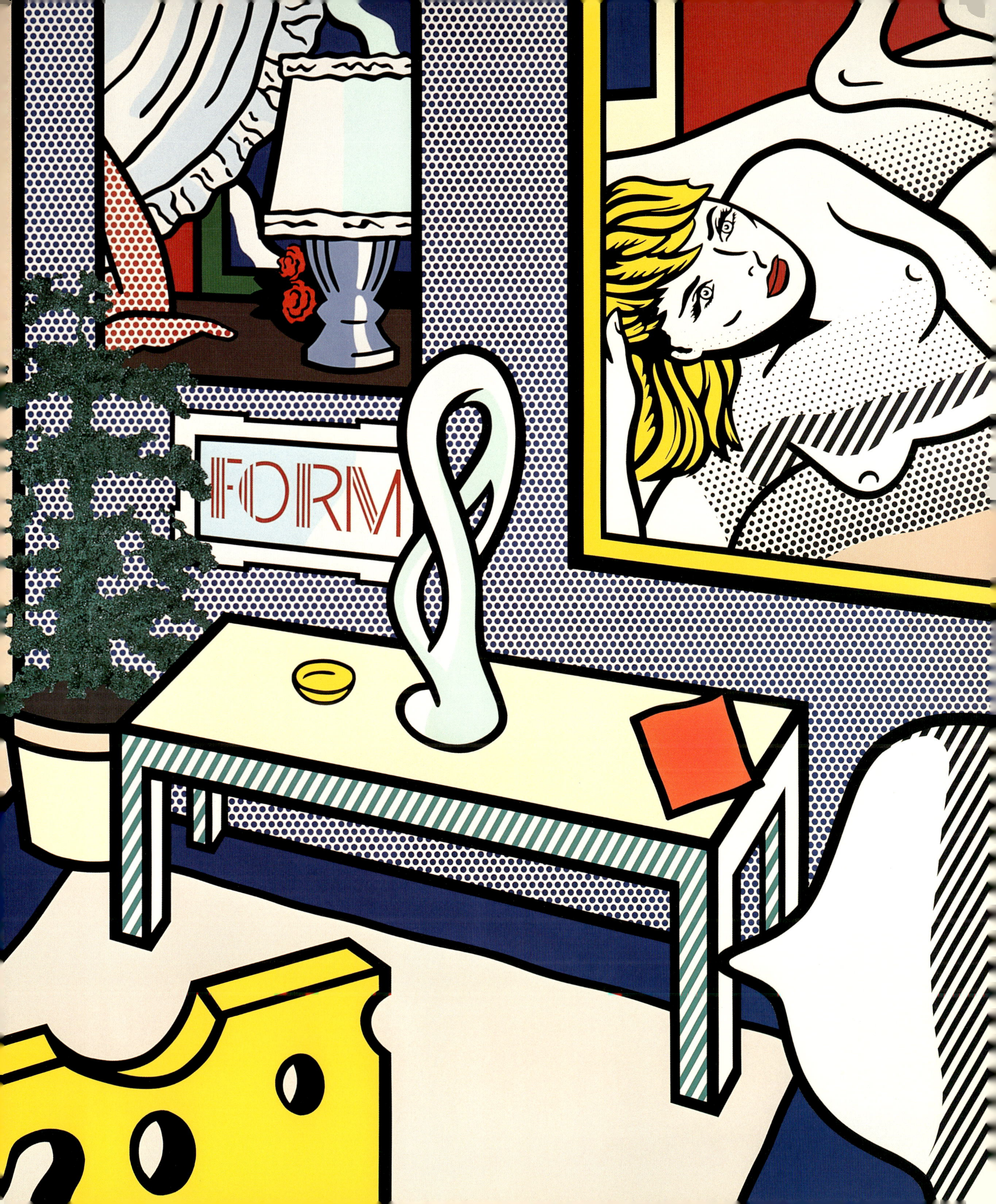
FORM

1 Clipping from Lichtenstein scrapbook (*The Flash,* no. 135 © 1963. DC Comics).

2 ***Imperfect Sculpture***, 1995. Cat. no. 52.

3 Clipping from Lichtenstein scrapbook (*The Incredible Hulk: Future Imperfect, #1* © Marvel Characters, Inc.).

RIGHT
Large Interior with Three Reflections (detail), 1993. Cat. no. 40.

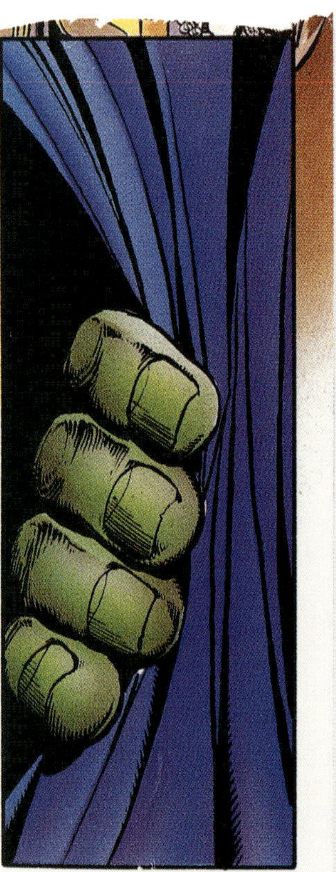

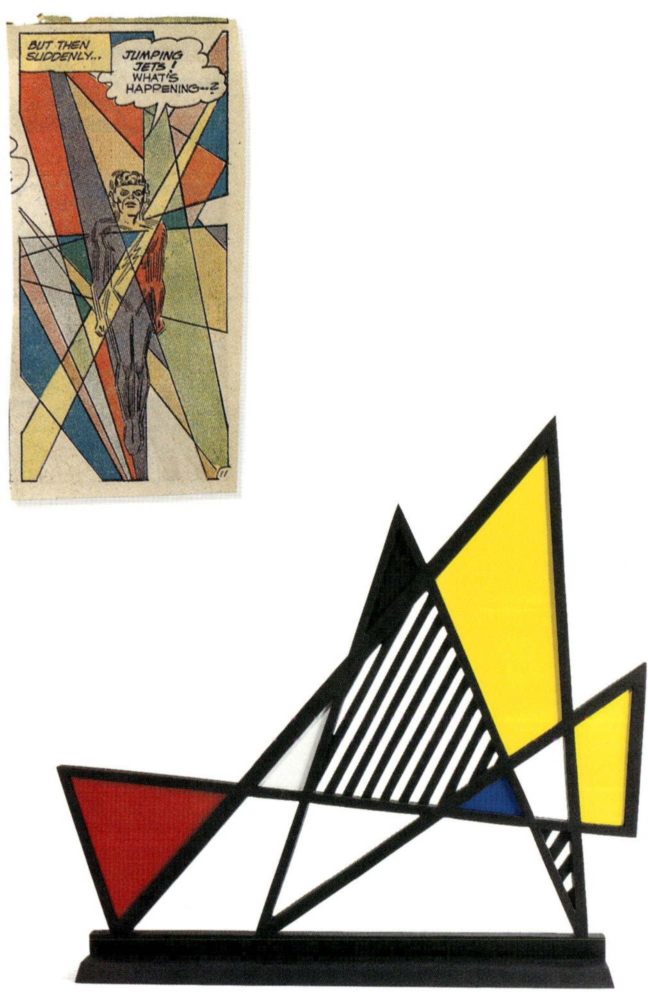

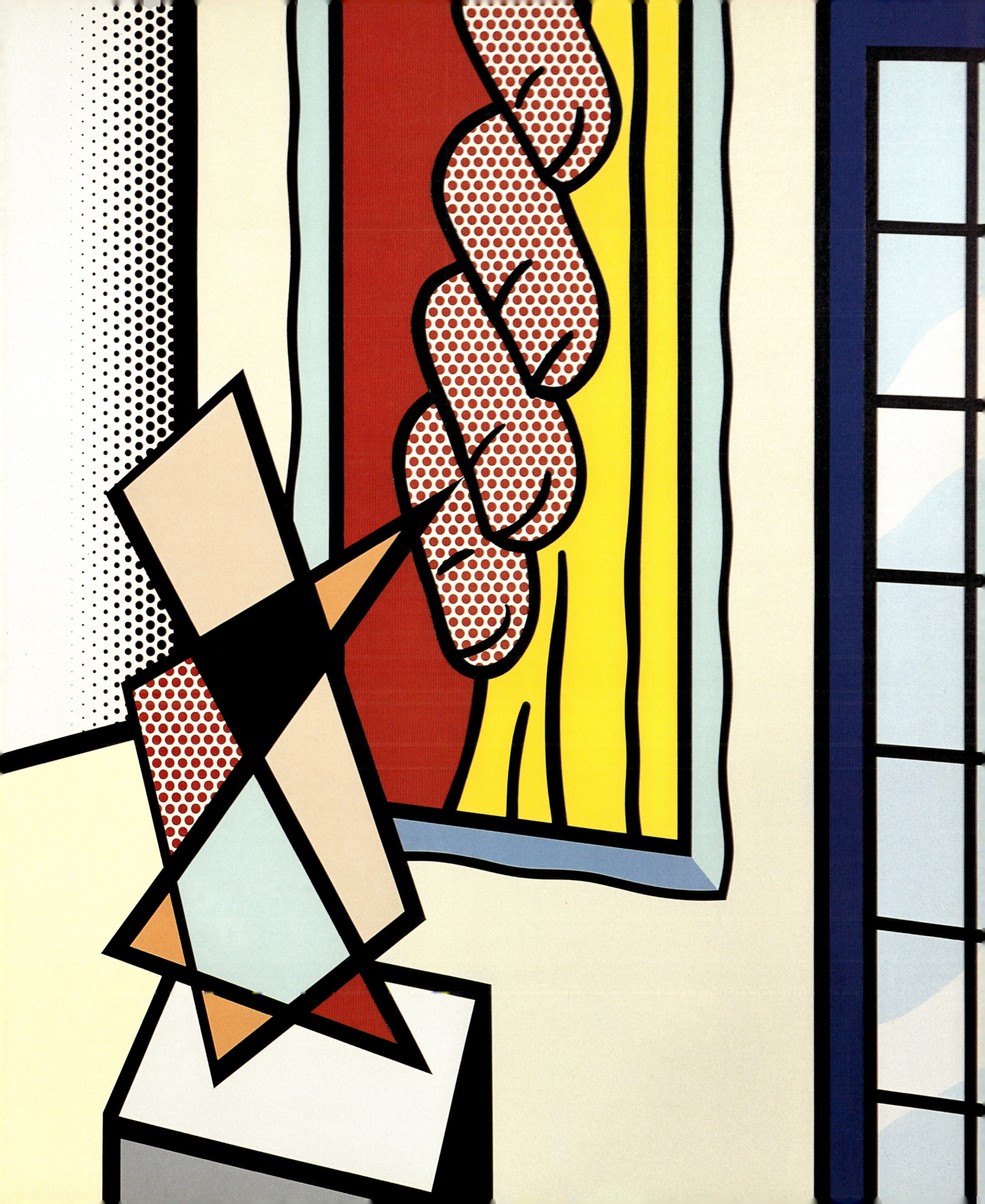

Interior with Exterior
(Still Waters), 1991.
Cat. no. 18.

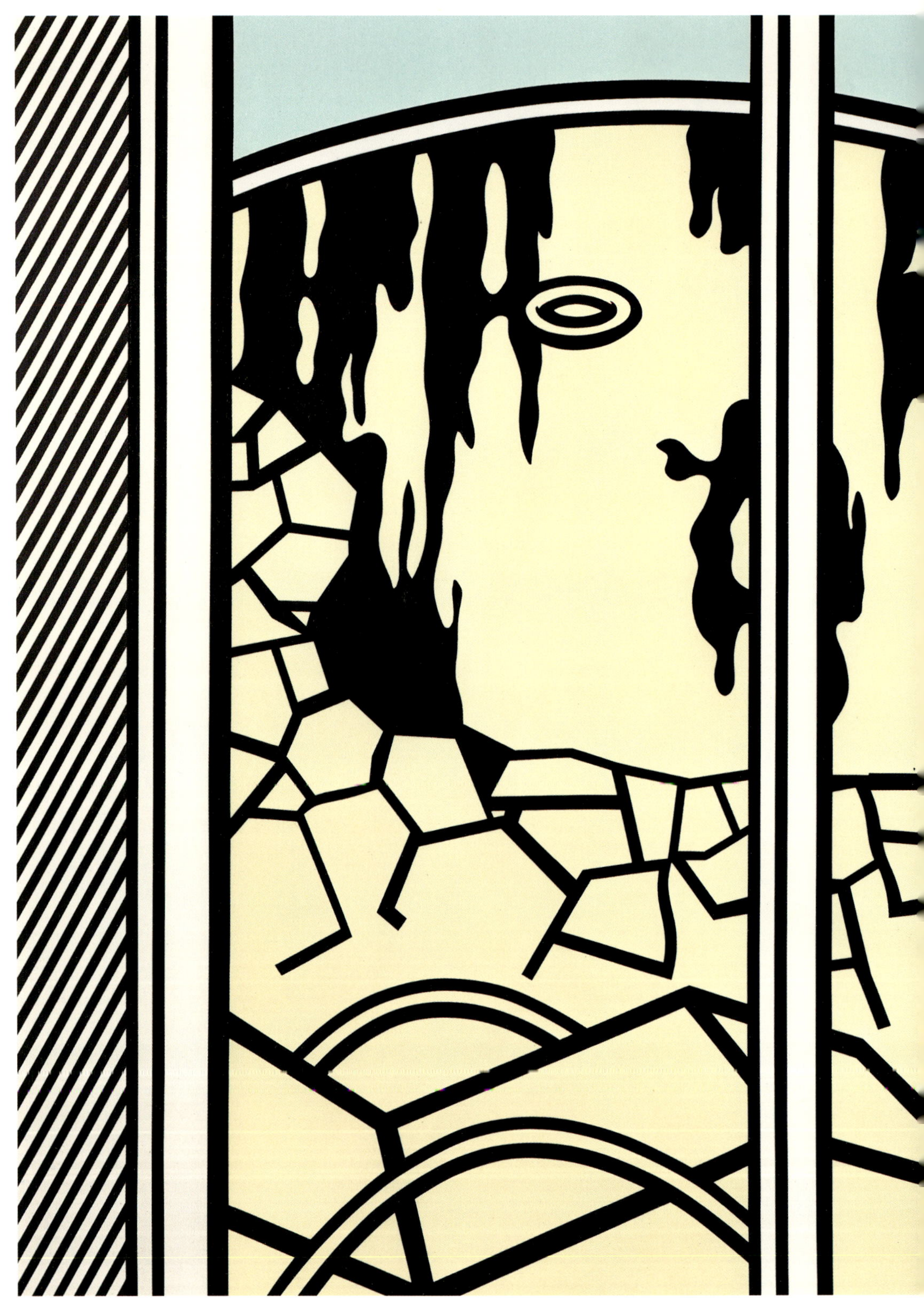

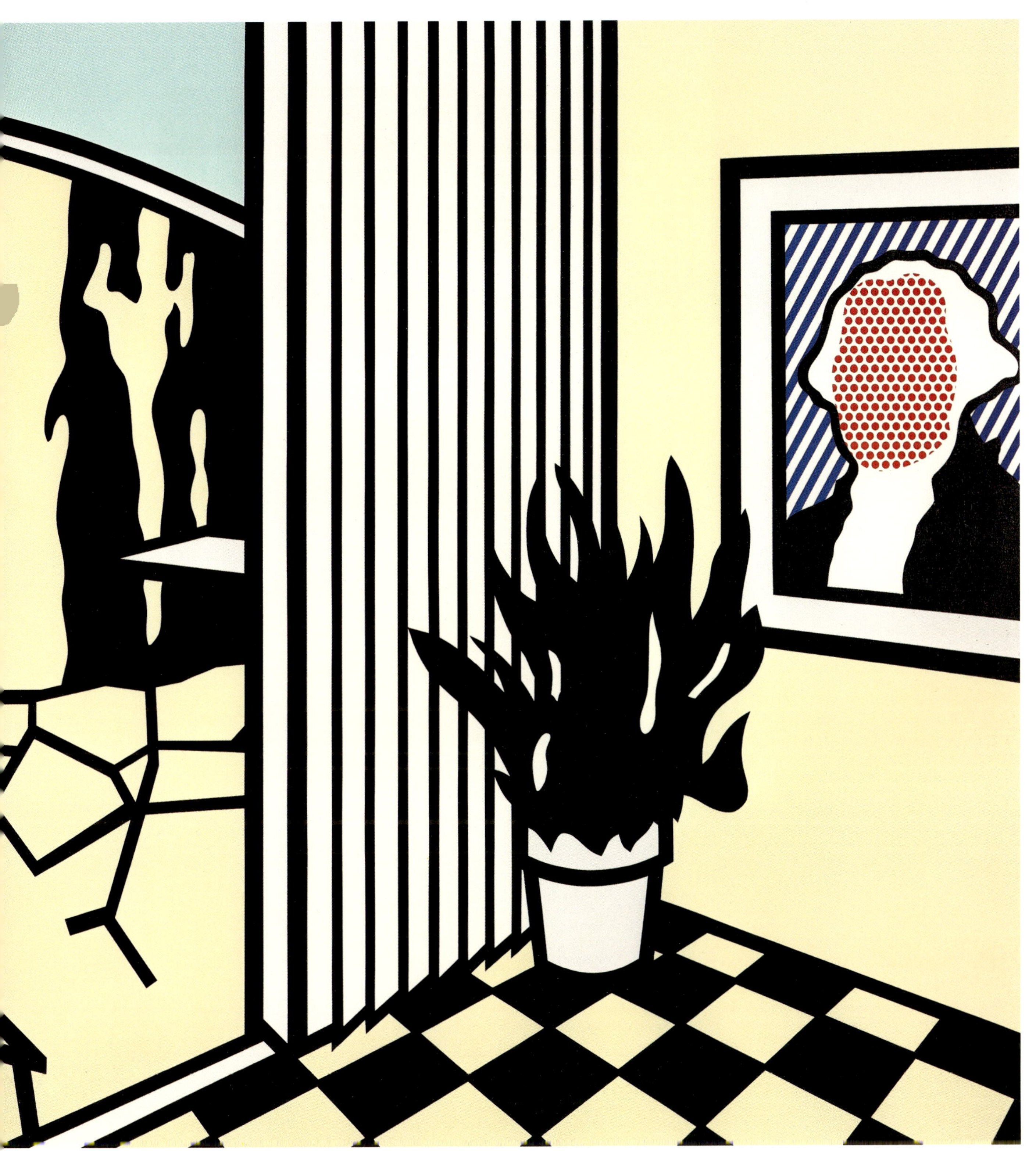

1

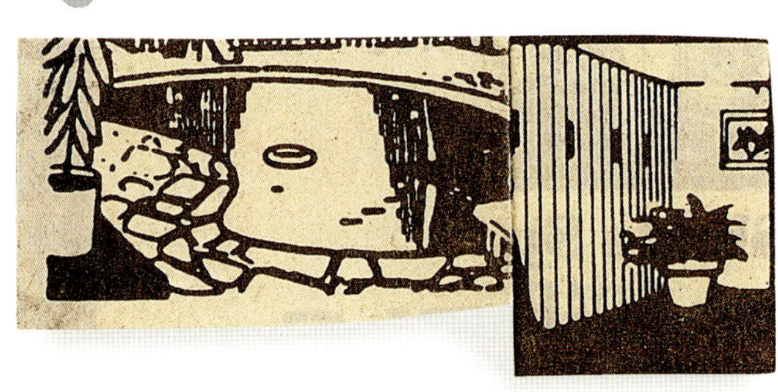

4

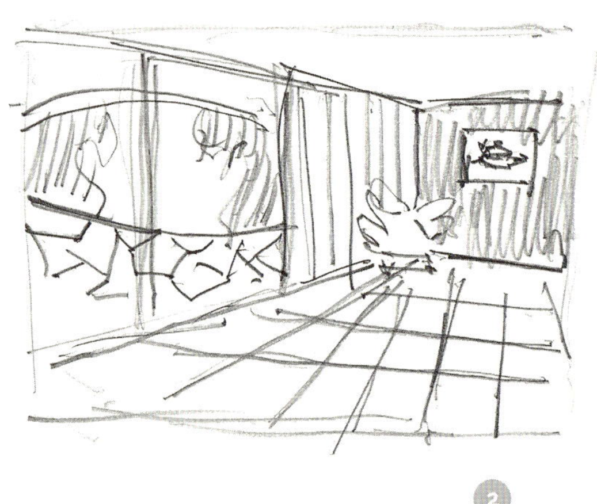

2

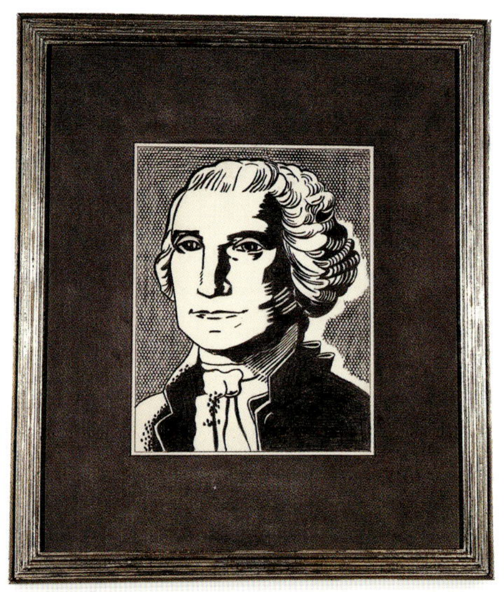

3

1 Clyfford Still, *1957-D No. 1*, 1957. Oil on canvas; 133 × 159 in. Albright-Knox Art Gallery, Buffalo, N.Y. Gift of Seymour H. Knox, 1959.

2 ***Interior with Exterior (Still Waters)*** (drawing for painting), 1991. Cat. no. 19.

3 ***George Washington*** (drawing for painting), 1962. Cat. no. 2.

4 Clipping from Lichtenstein scrapbook.

RIGHT
Interior with Exterior (Still Waters) (collage for painting), 1991. Cat. no. 20.

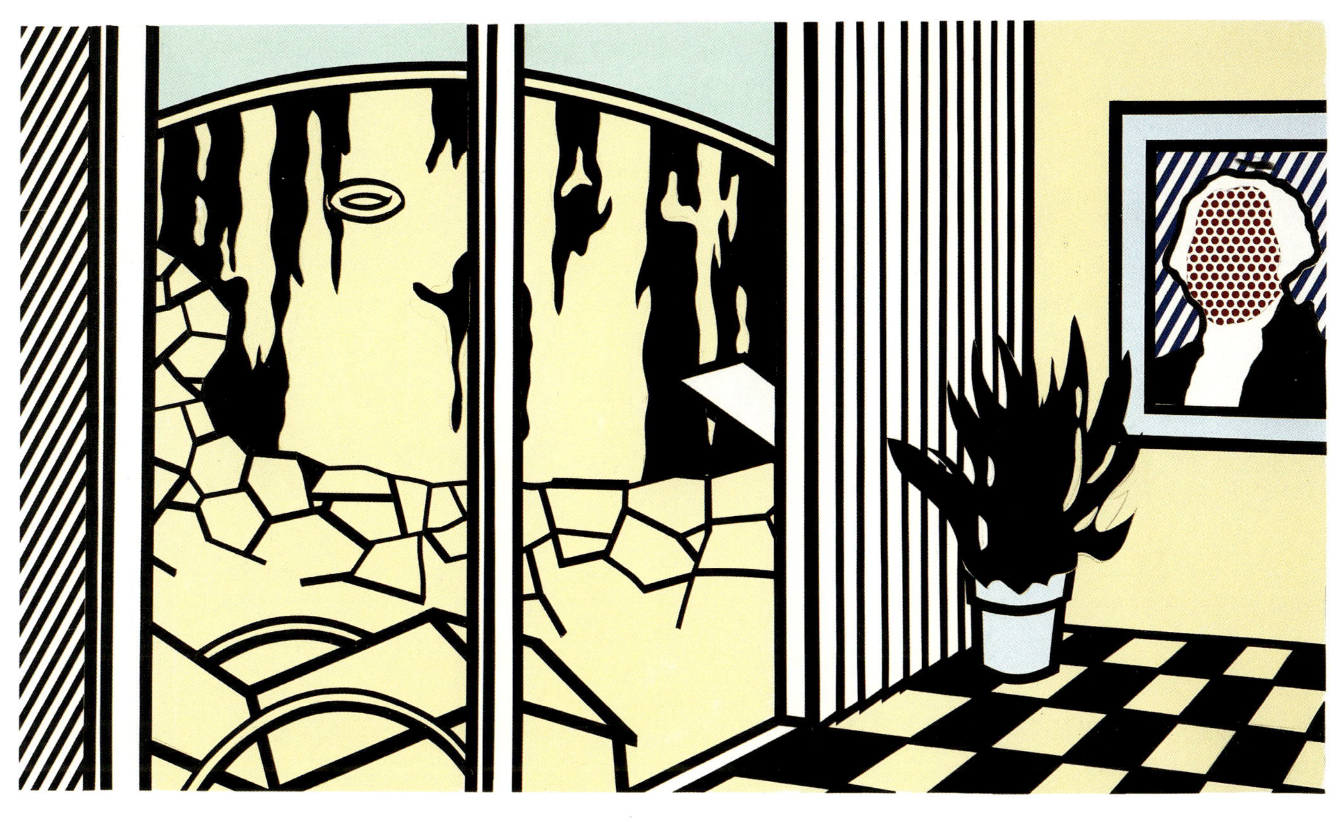

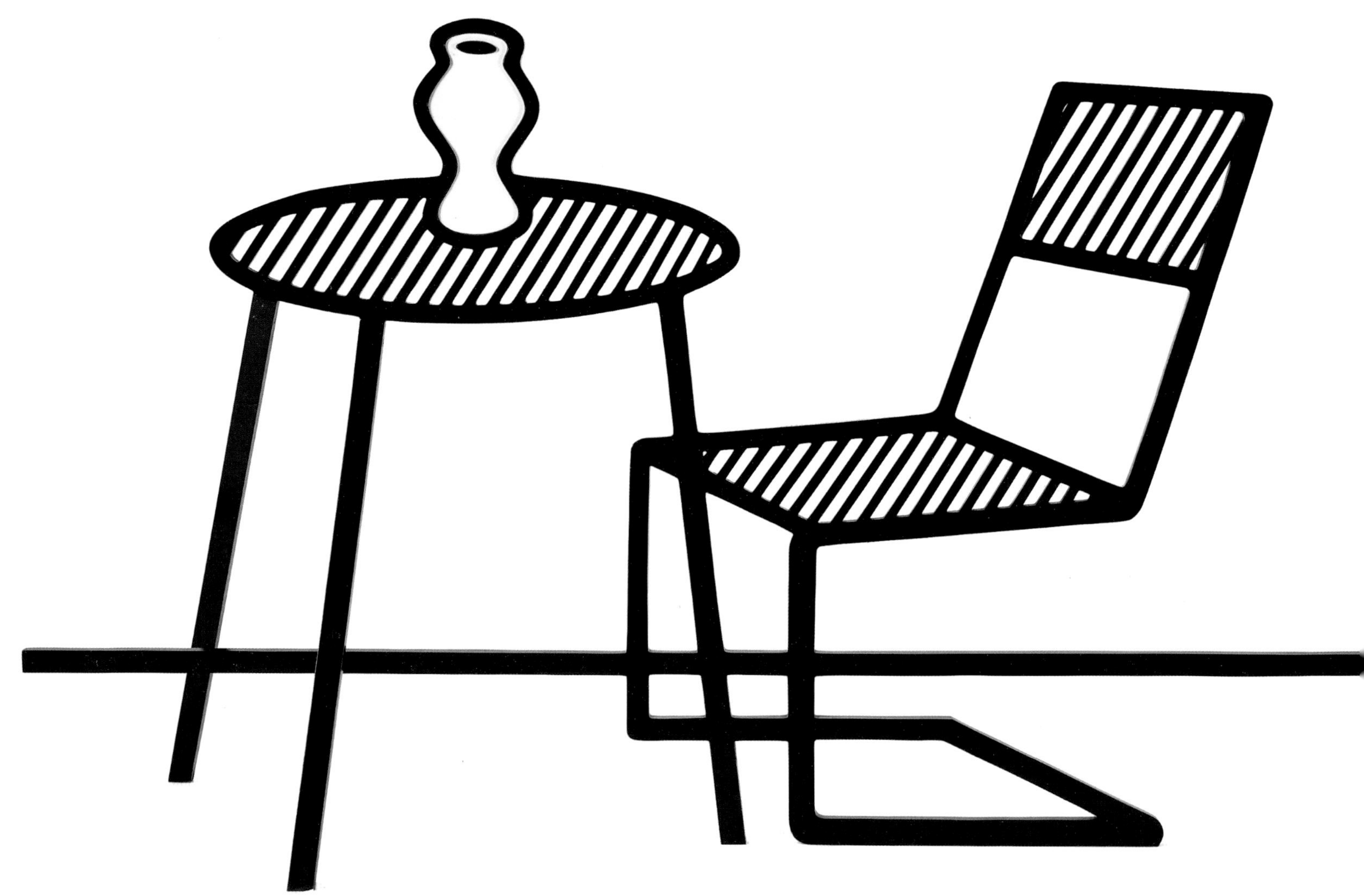

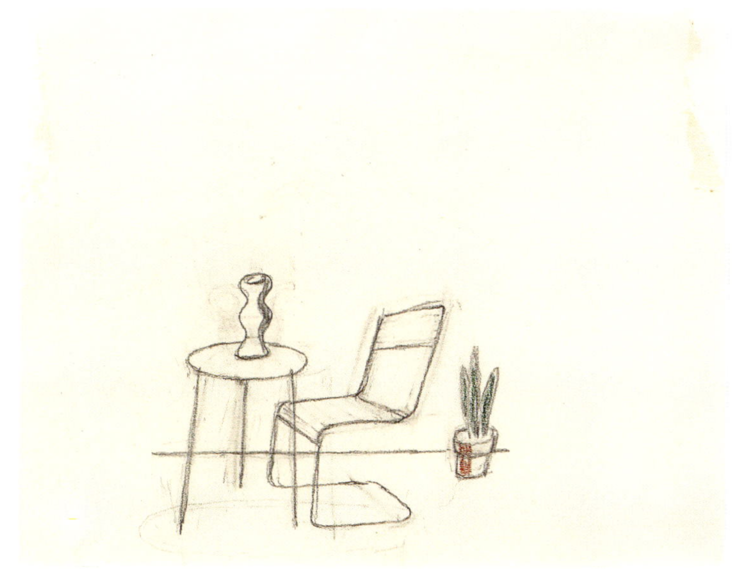

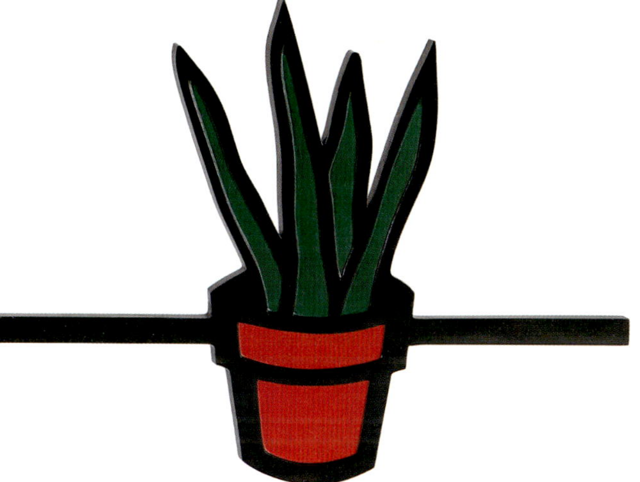

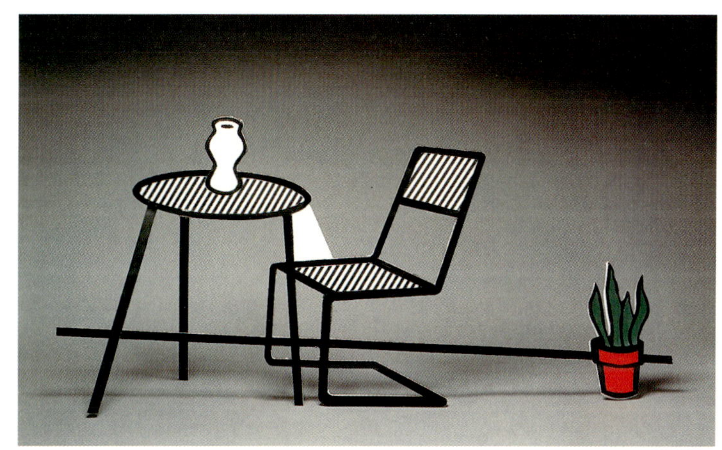

Untitled (drawing), 1976. Cat. no. 7.

Chair, Table, and Flower Pot (maquette for sculpture), 1992. Cat. no. 28.

LEFT
Chair, Table, and Flower Pot, 1993. Cat. no. 34.

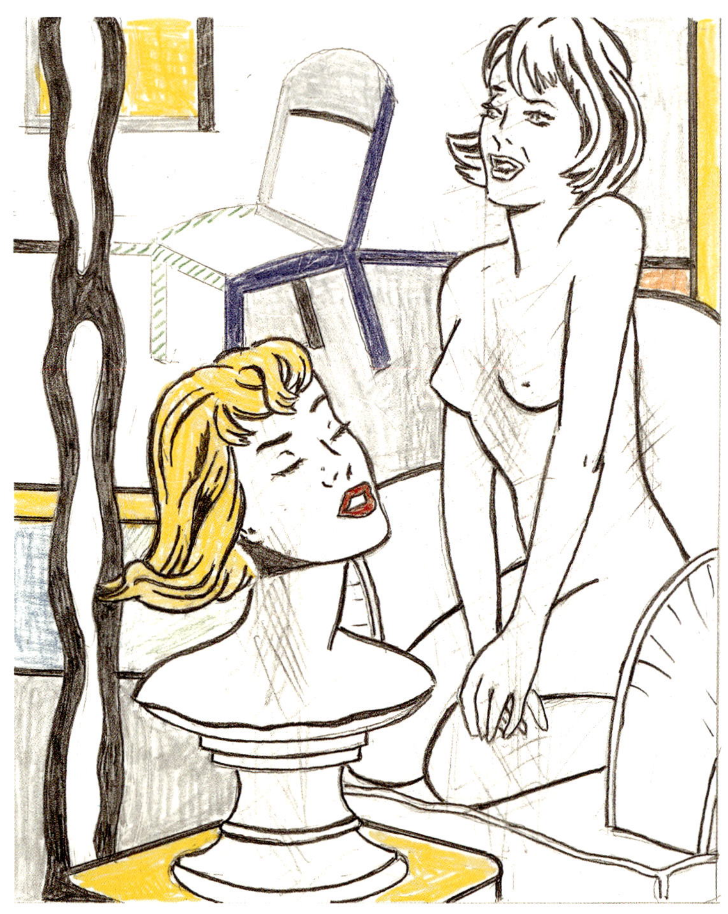

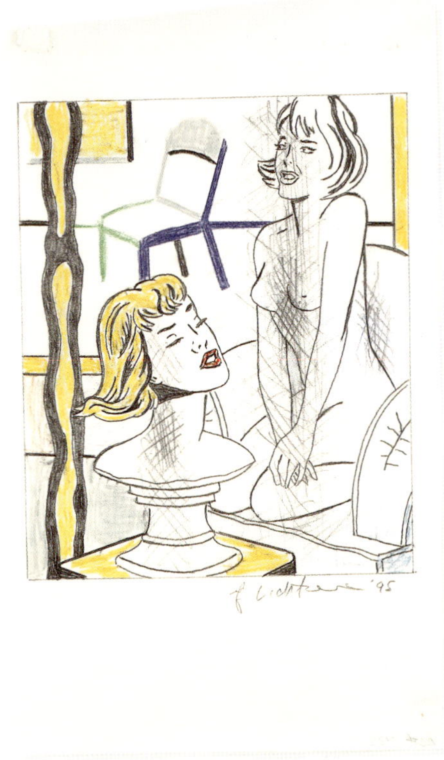

Nude with Bust
(drawing for painting),
1995. Cat. no. 55.

Nude with Bust
(drawing for painting),
1995. Cat. no. 57.

RIGHT
Nude with Bust
(collage for painting),
1995. Cat. no. 54.

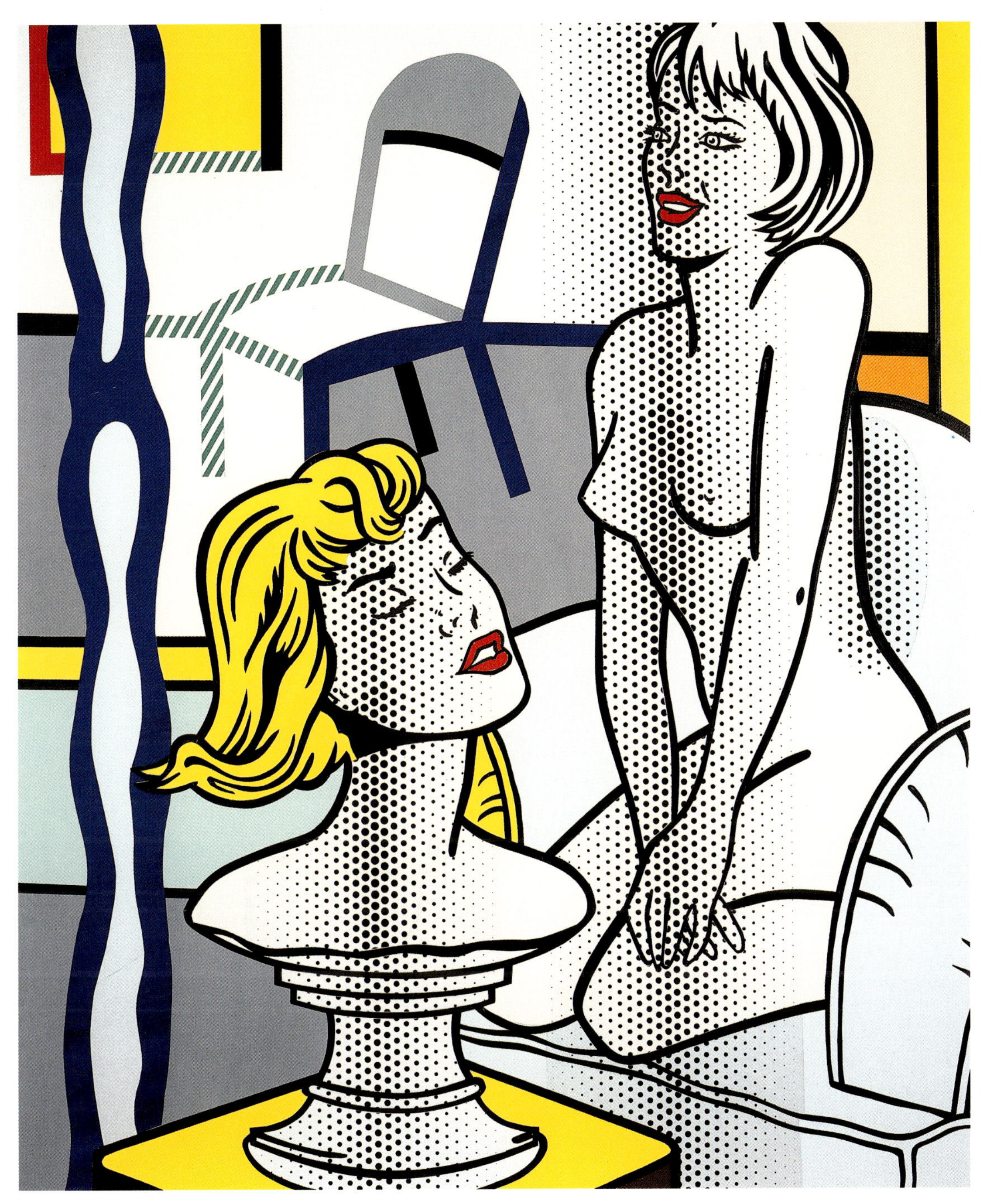

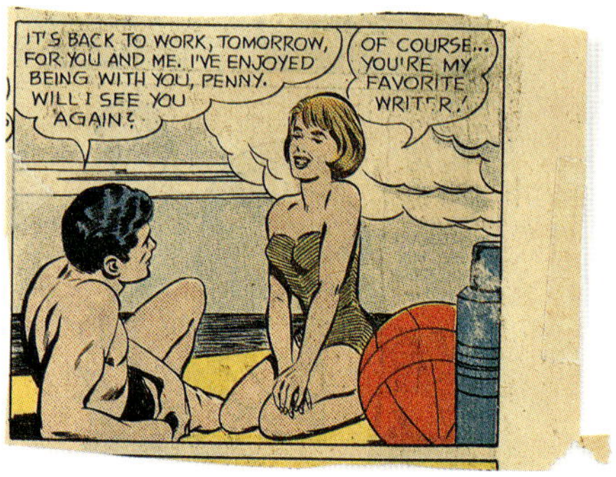

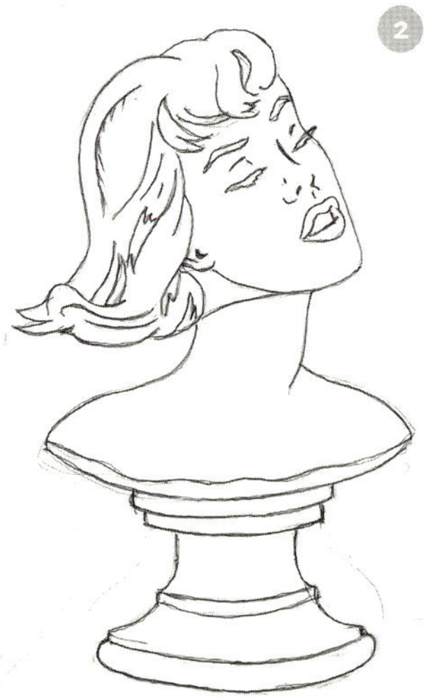

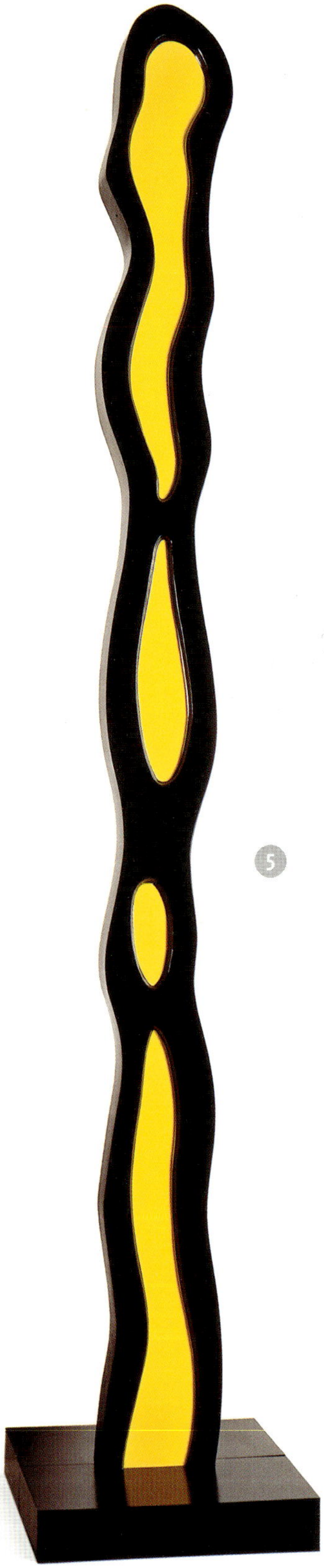

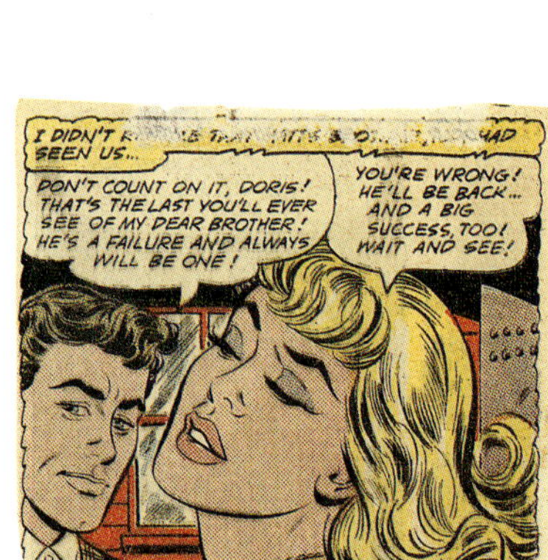

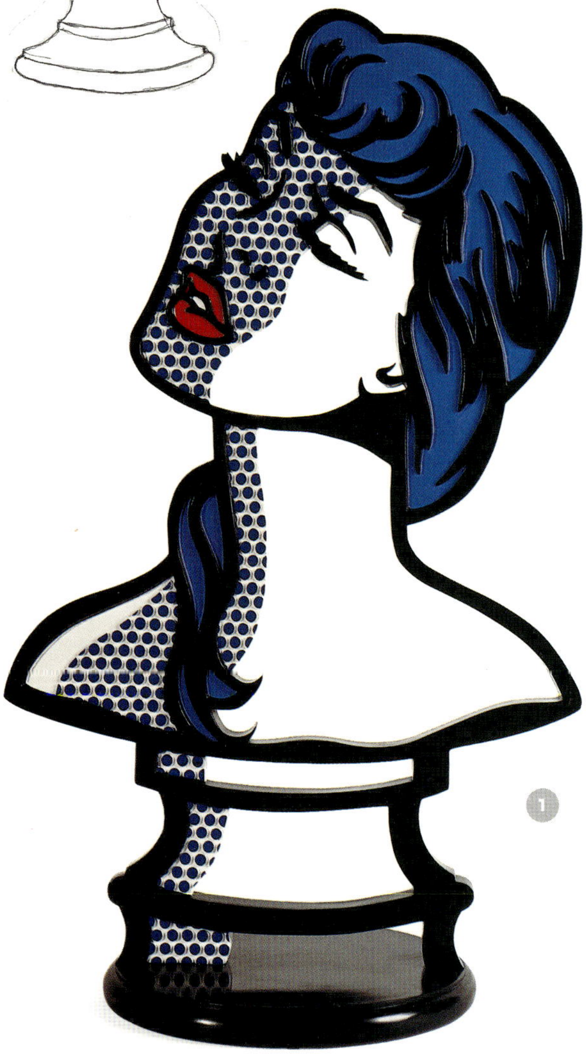

1 ***Woman: Sunlight, Moonlight***, 1996. Cat. no. 59.

2 ***Nude with Bust*** (sketch for painting), 1995. Cat. no. 56.

3 Clipping from Lichtenstein scrapbook (*Secret Hearts*, no. 95 © 1964 DC Comics).

4 Clipping from Lichtenstein scrapbook (*Young Romance*, no. 127 © 1964 DC Comics).

5 ***Endless Drip***, 1995. Cat. no. 51.

RIGHT
Nude With Bust, 1995. Cat. no. 53.

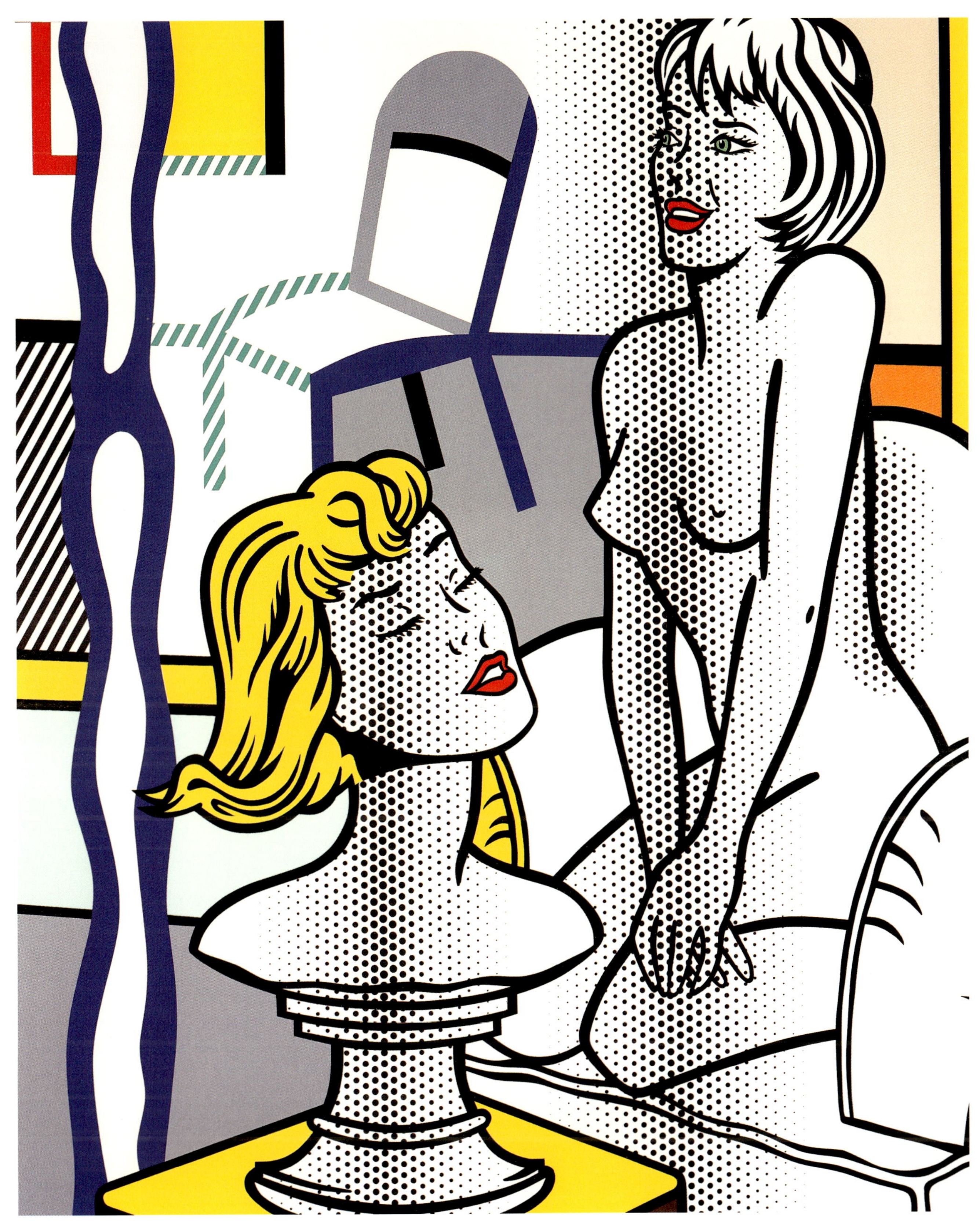

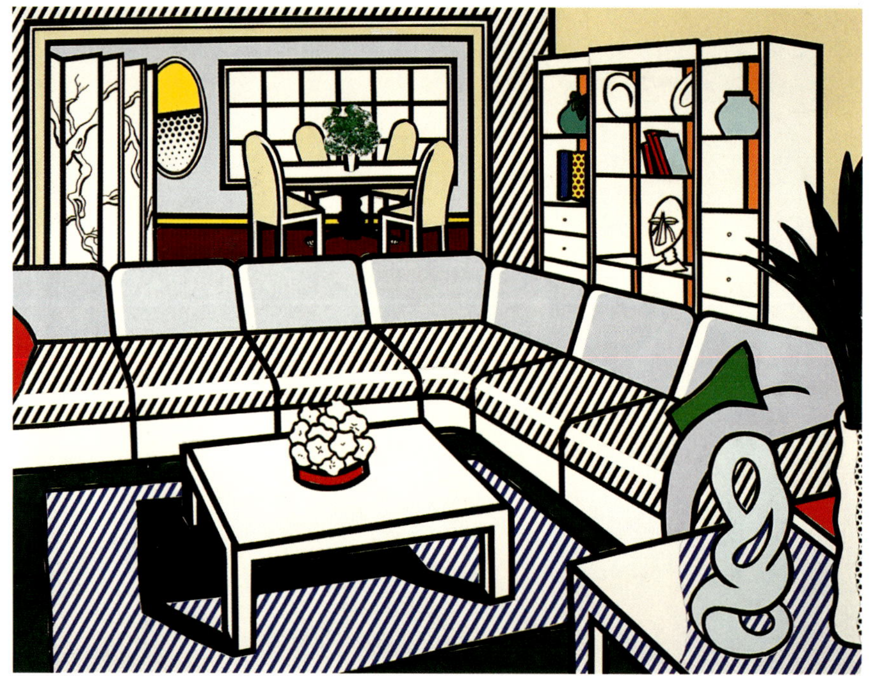

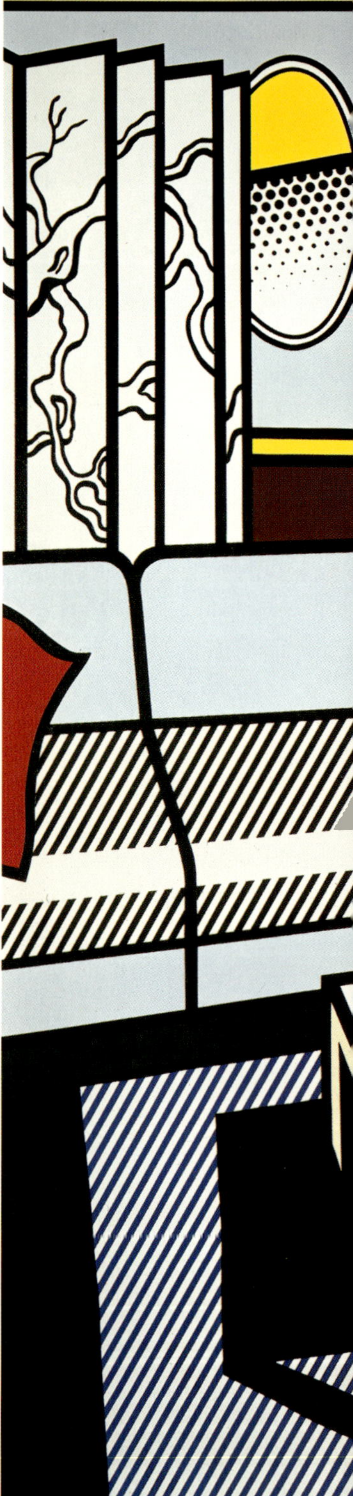

Interior with African Mask (collage for painting), 1991. Cat. no. 15.

RIGHT
Interior with African Mask, 1991. Cat. no. 14.

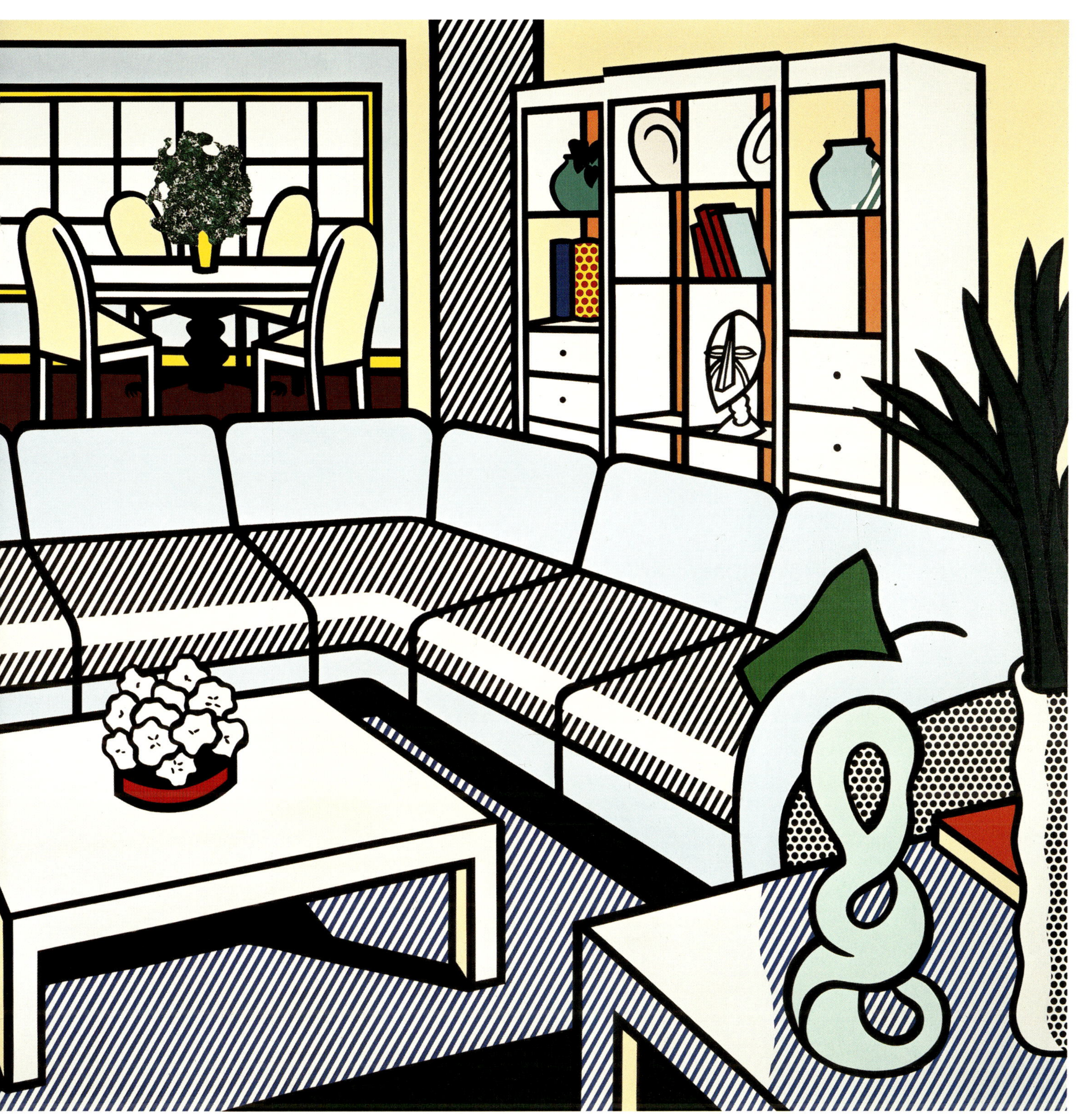

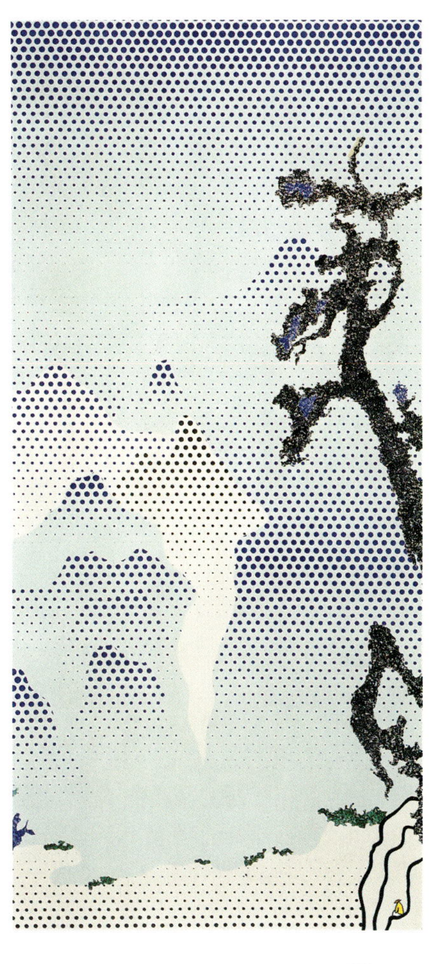

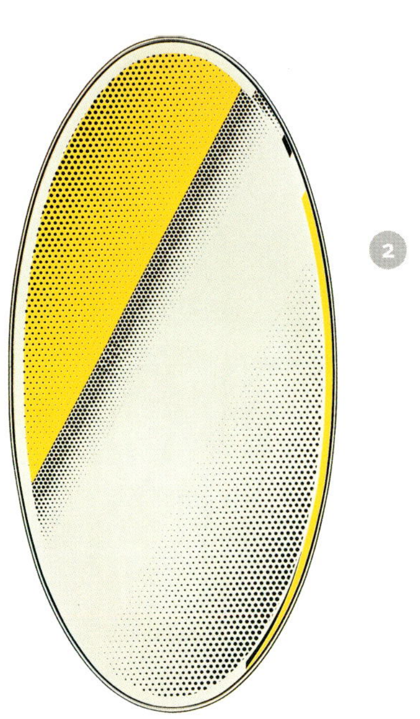

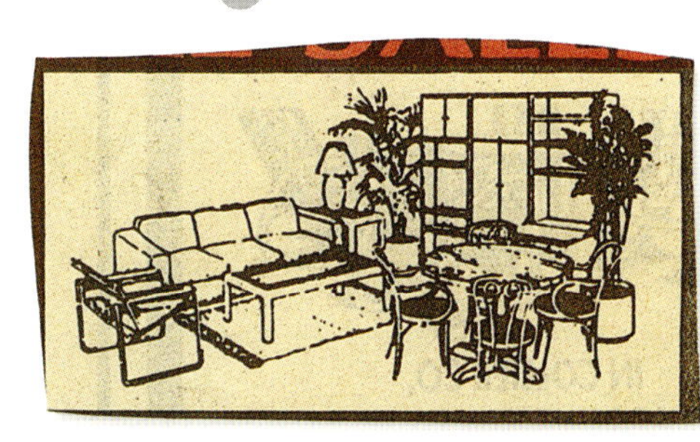

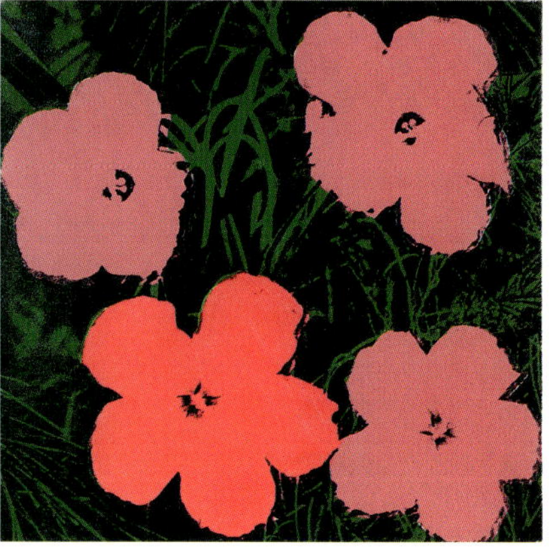

1 *Landscape with Philosopher,* 1996. Oil and Magna on canvas; 104 × 47 3/4 in. Private collection, New York.

2 ***Oval Mirror 6' × 3' #3***, 1971. Cat. no. 3.

3 Andy Warhol, *Flowers,* 1964. Oil and silkscreen on canvas; 24 × 24 in. Private collection, New York © 2001 Andy Warhol Foundation for the Visual Arts/ARS, New York. Photo courtesy of Anthony d'Offay Gallery, London.

4 Clipping from Lichtenstein scrapbook.

RIGHT
Interior with African Mask, (detail) 1991. Cat. no. 14.

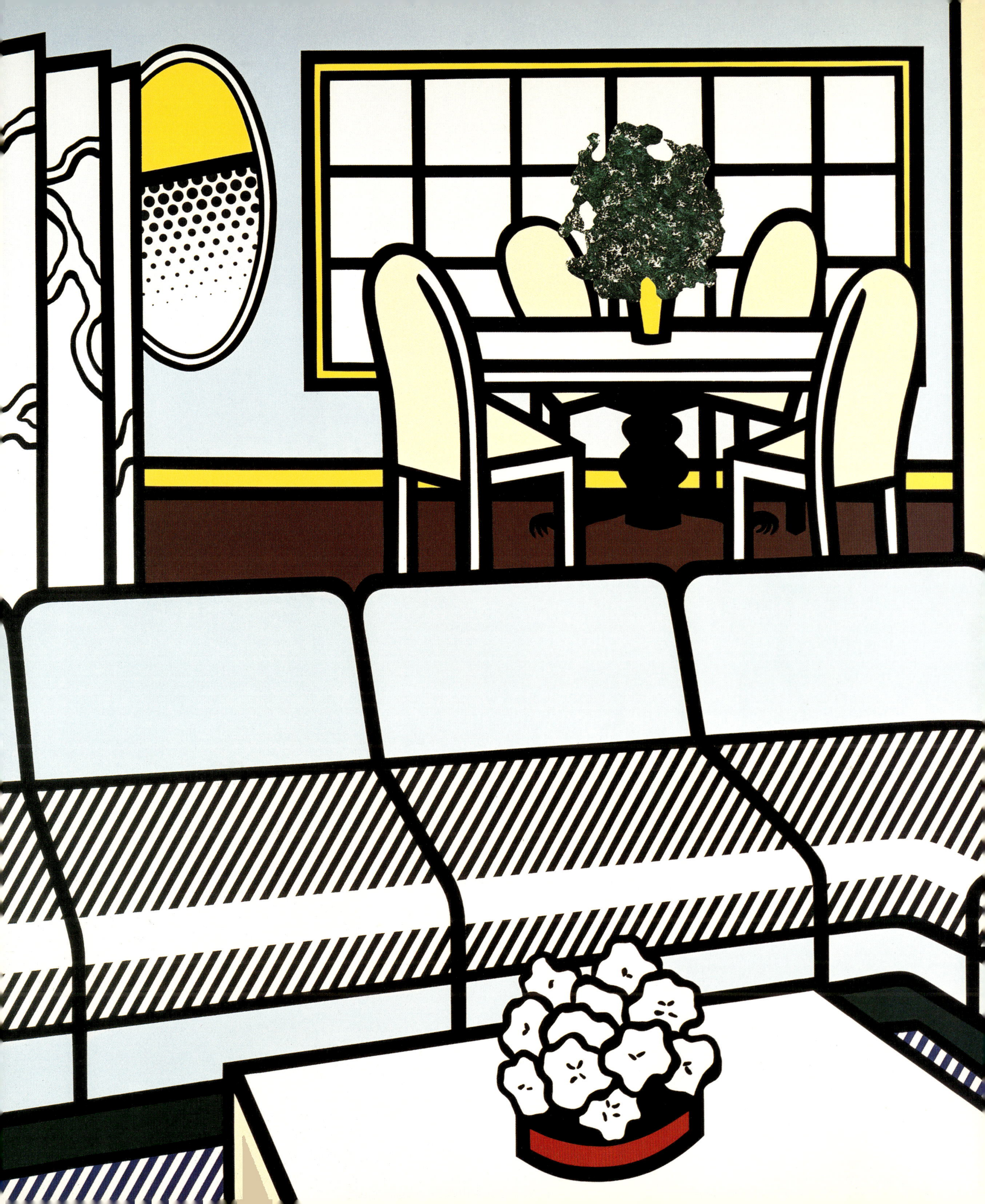

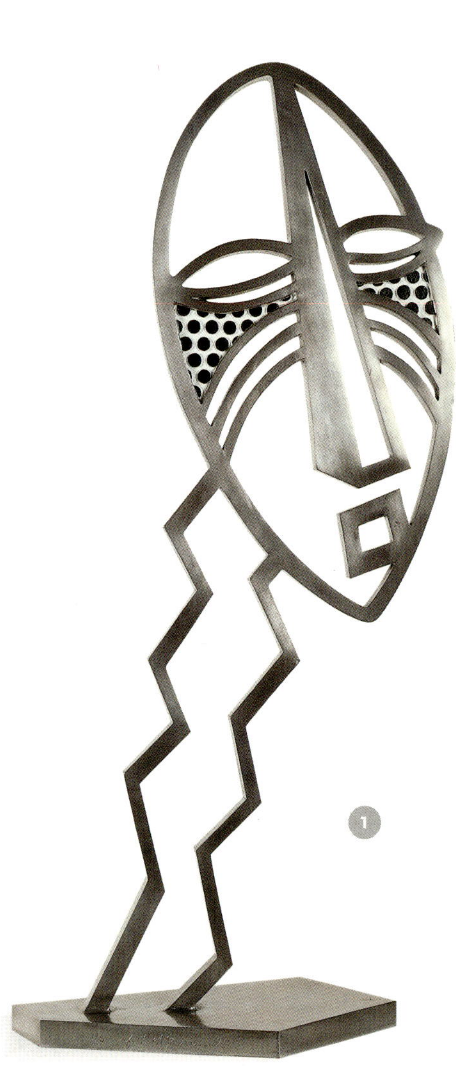

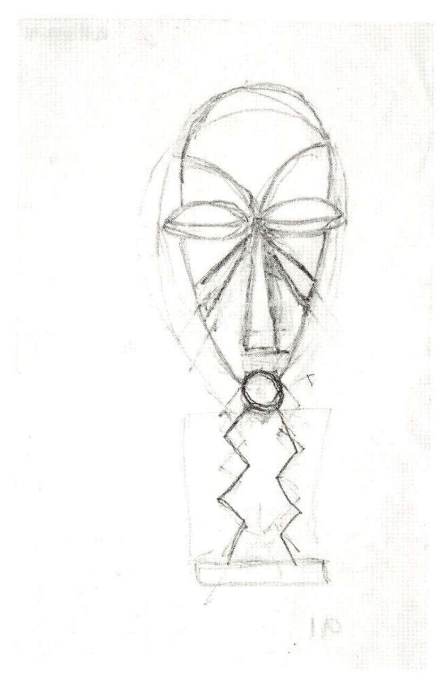

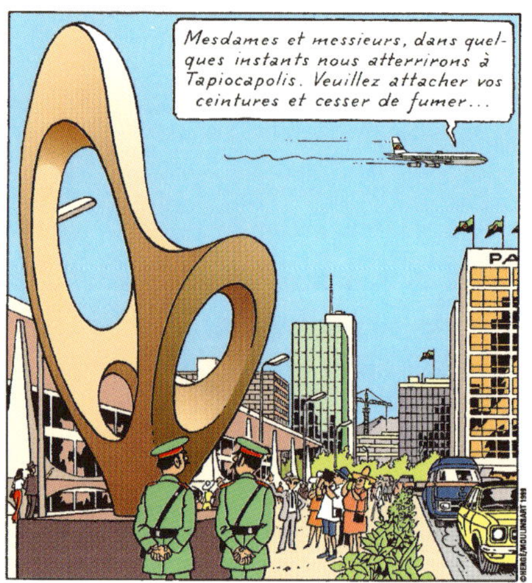

1 ***Ritual Mask,*** 1992. Cat. no. 31.

2 ***Ritual Mask*** (study for sculpture), 1992. Cat. no. 32.

3 Clipping from Lichtenstein scrapbook (*Tintin and the Picaros* © Hergé/Moulinsart 2001).

RIGHT
Interior with African Mask (detail), 1991. Cat. no. 14.

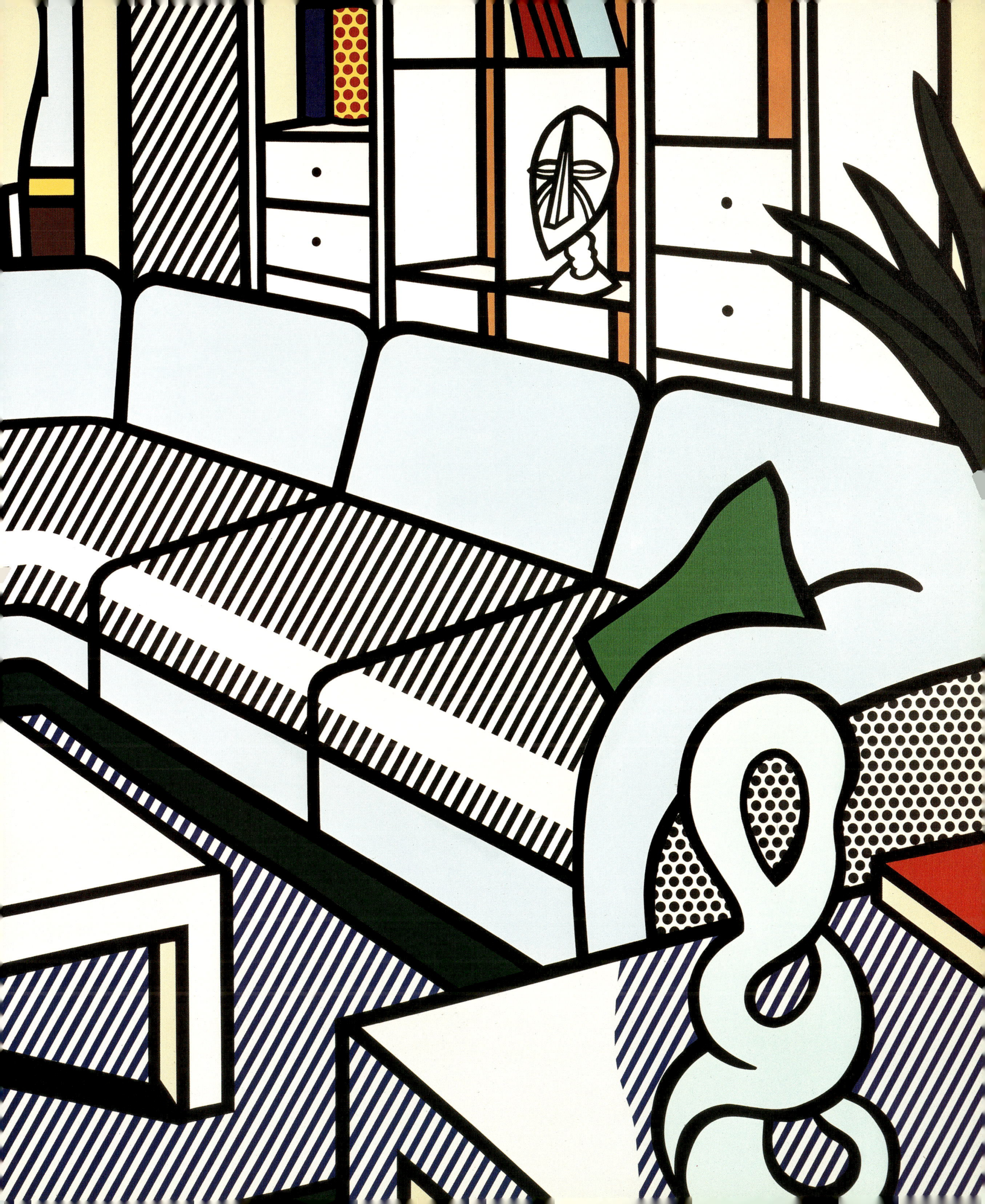

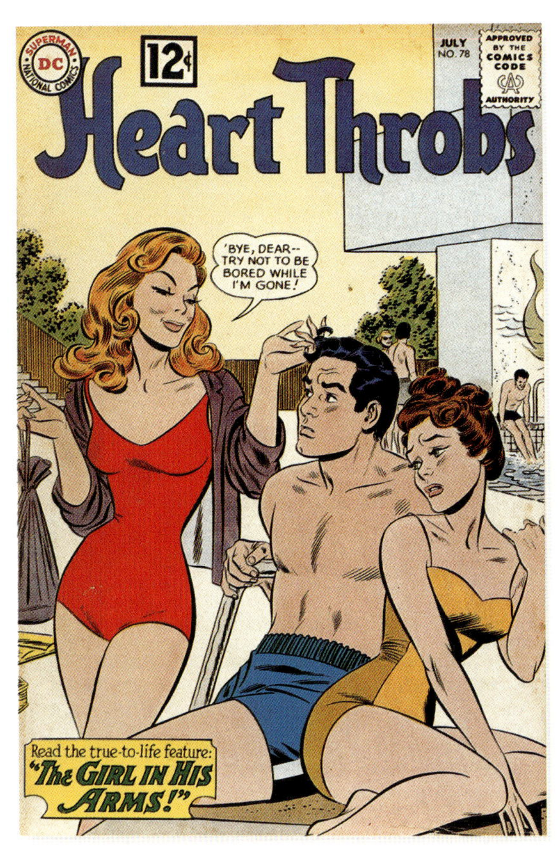

Clipping from Lichtenstein scrapbook (*Heart Throbs*, no. 78 © 1962 DC Comics).

RIGHT
Blue Nude, 1995.
Cat. no. 49.

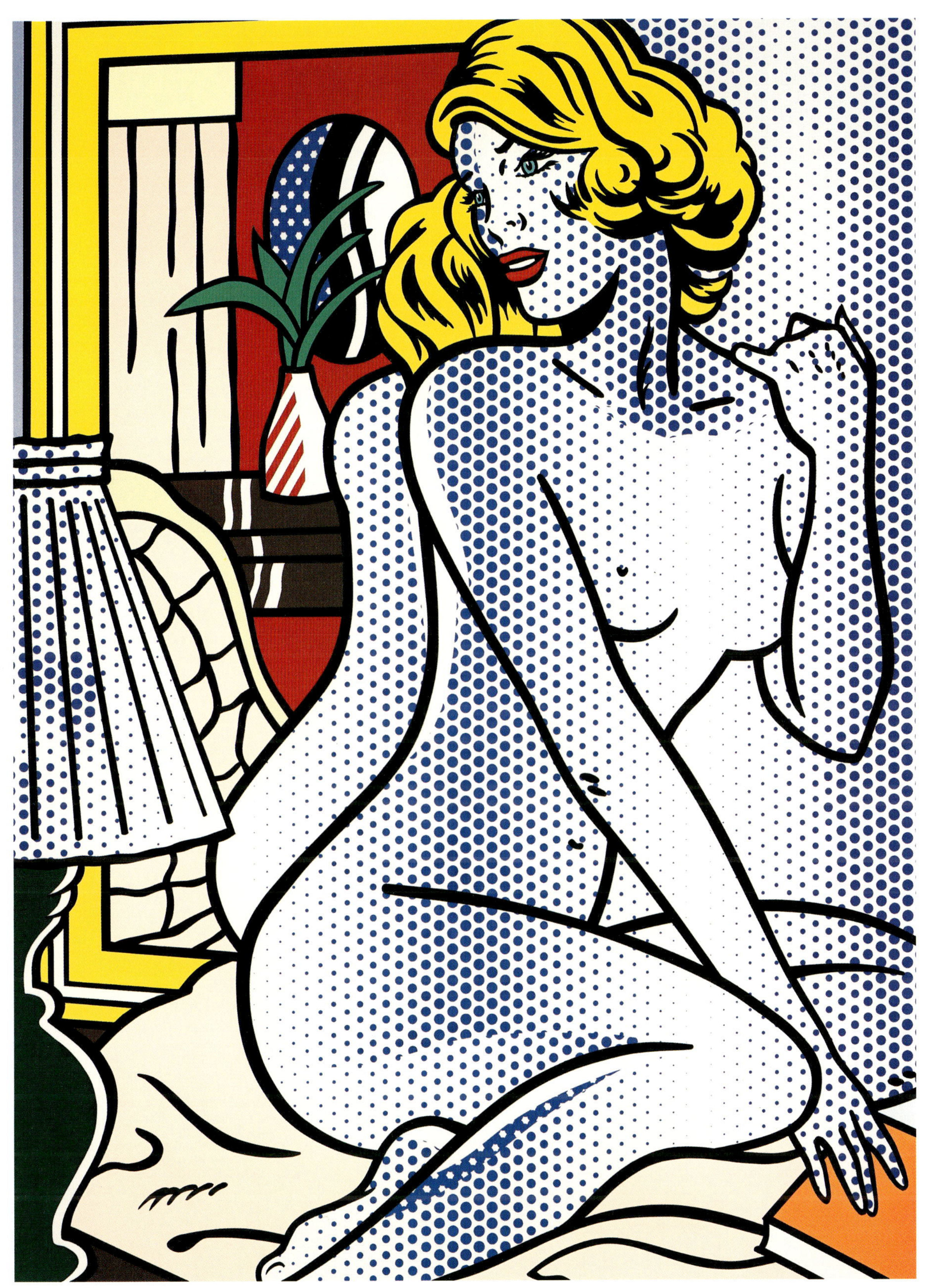

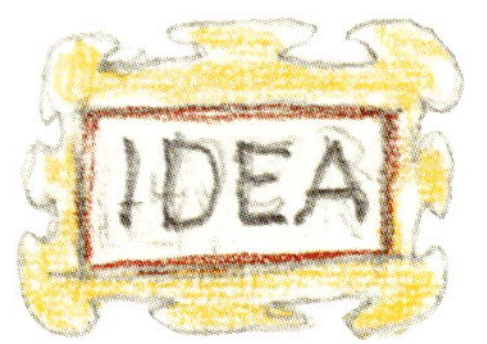

5

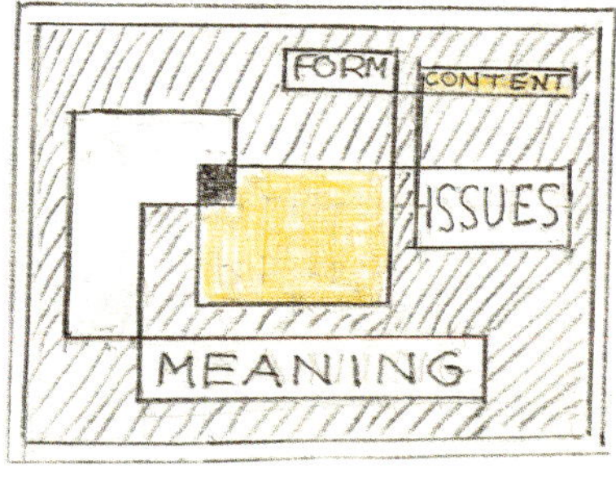

1

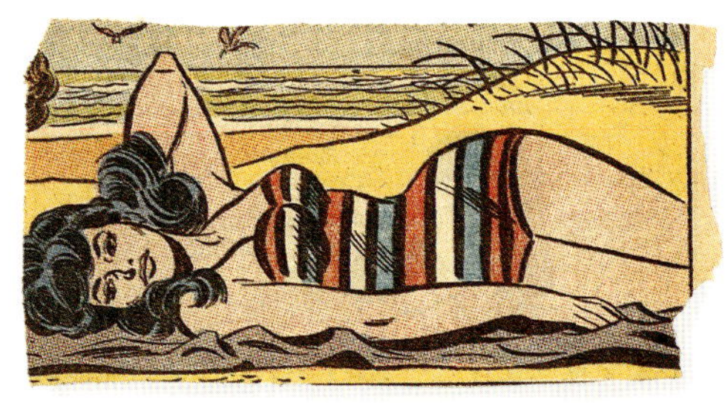

4

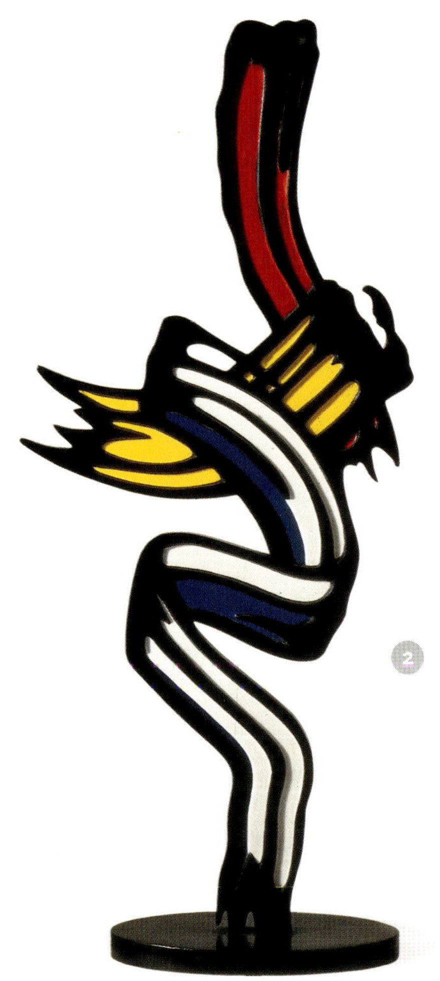

2

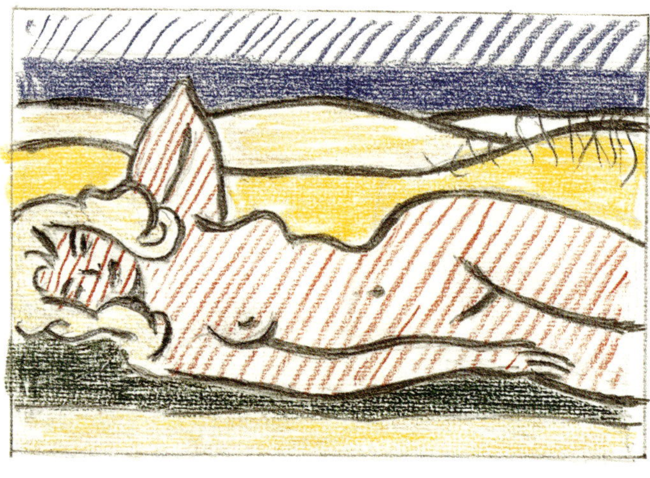

3

1 ***Idea*** (sketch for painting) (detail), 1993. Cat. no. 36.

2 *Brushstroke*, 1981. Polyurethane enamel and Magna on patinated bronze; 31 3/8 × 13 3/4 × 6 1/2 in. Private collection.

3 ***Idea*** (drawing for painting) (detail), 1993. Cat. no. 37.

4 Clipping from Lichtenstein scrapbook (*Heart Throbs*, no. 78 © 1962 DC Comics).

5 ***Idea*** (sketch for painting) (detail), 1993. Cat. no. 36.

RIGHT
Idea, 1993. Cat. no. 35.

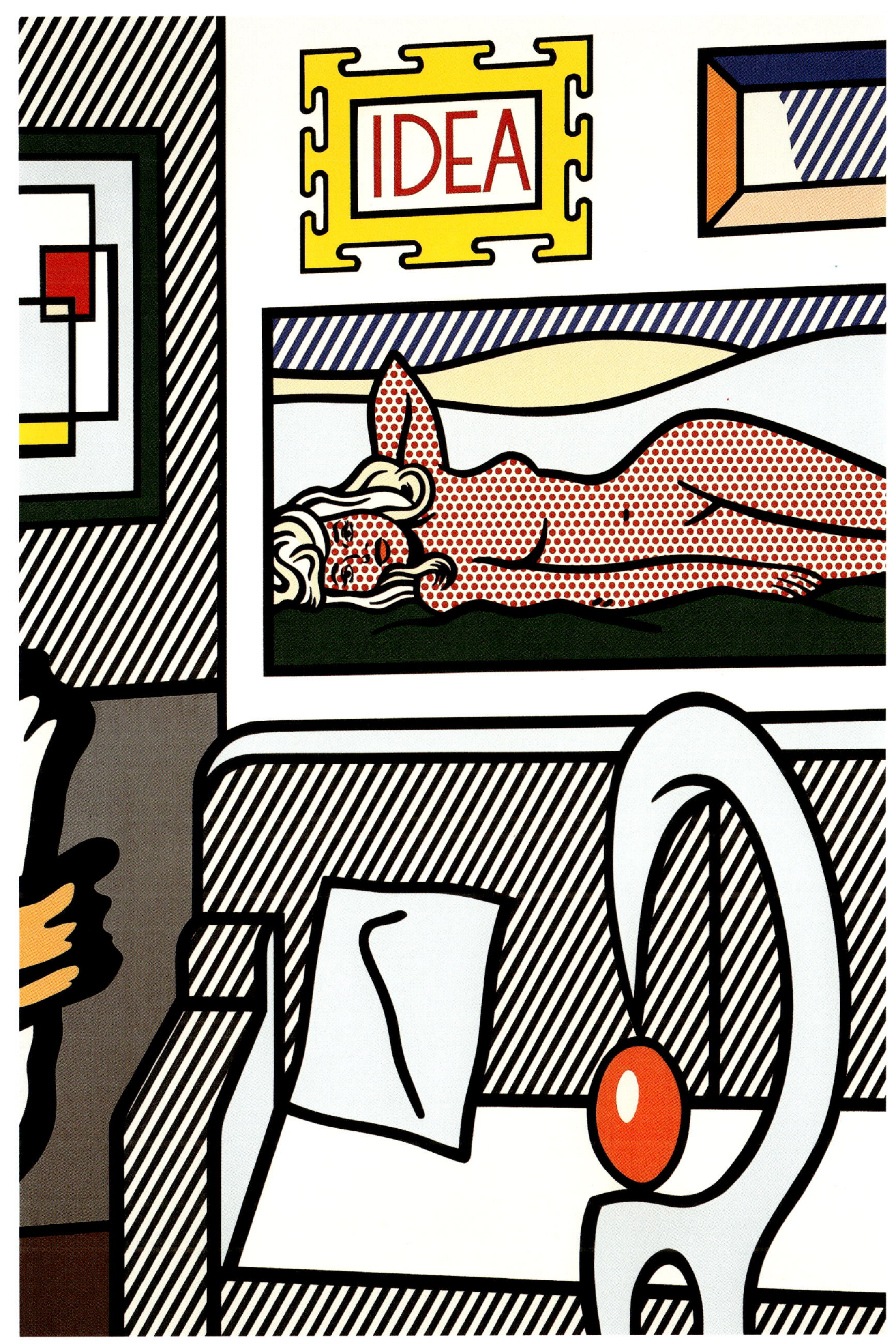
IDEA

1 *Unchained Melody*, 1994. Oil and Magna on canvas; 70 in. x 62 in. Private collection, New York.

2 ***Interior: Perfect Pitcher*** (drawing for painting), 1994. Cat. no. 46.

3 Clipping from Lichtenstein scrapbook.

4 Clipping from Lichtenstein scrapbook (*Falling in Love*, no. 59 © 1963 DC Comics).

RIGHT
Interior: Perfect Pitcher, 1994. Cat. no. 45.

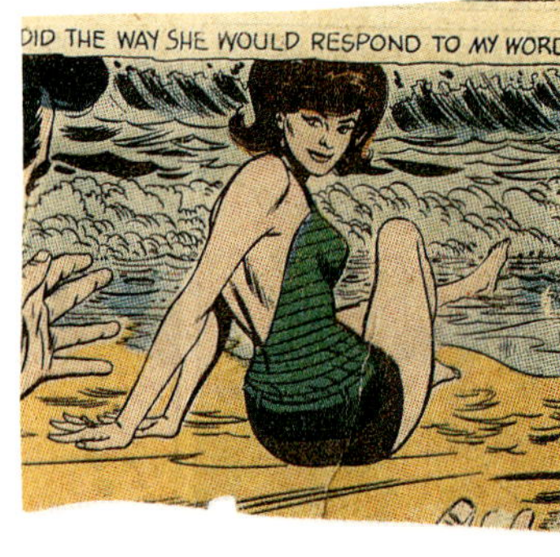

4

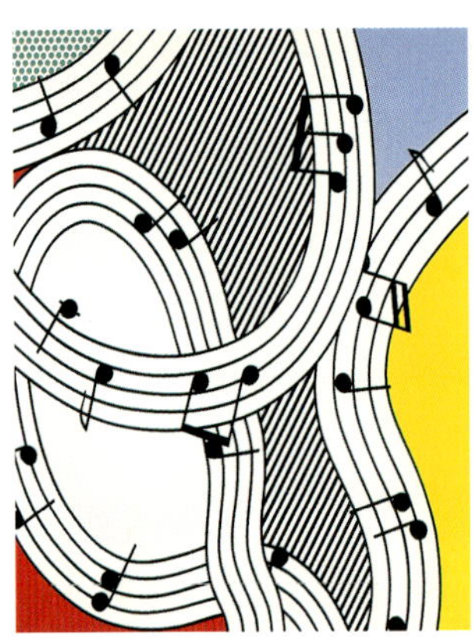

1

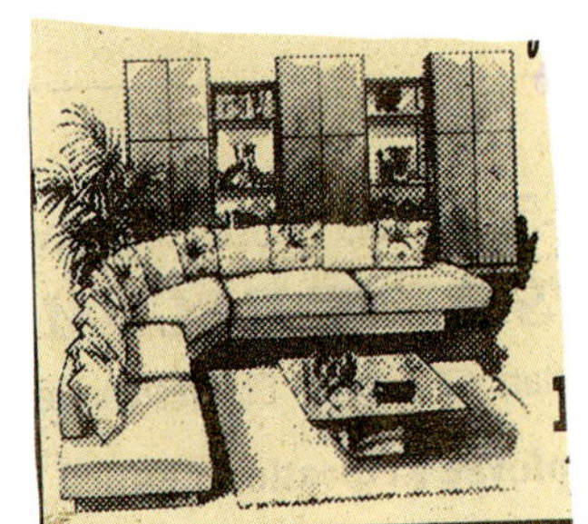

3

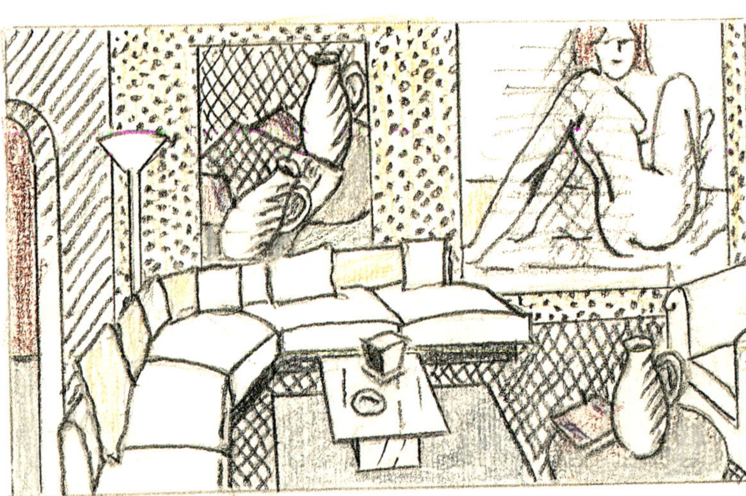

2

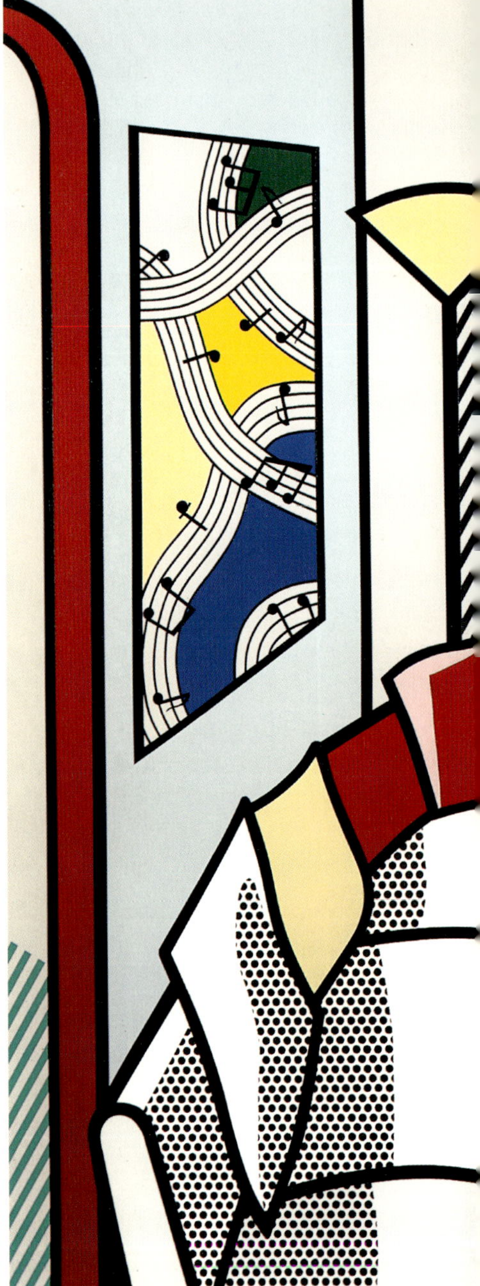

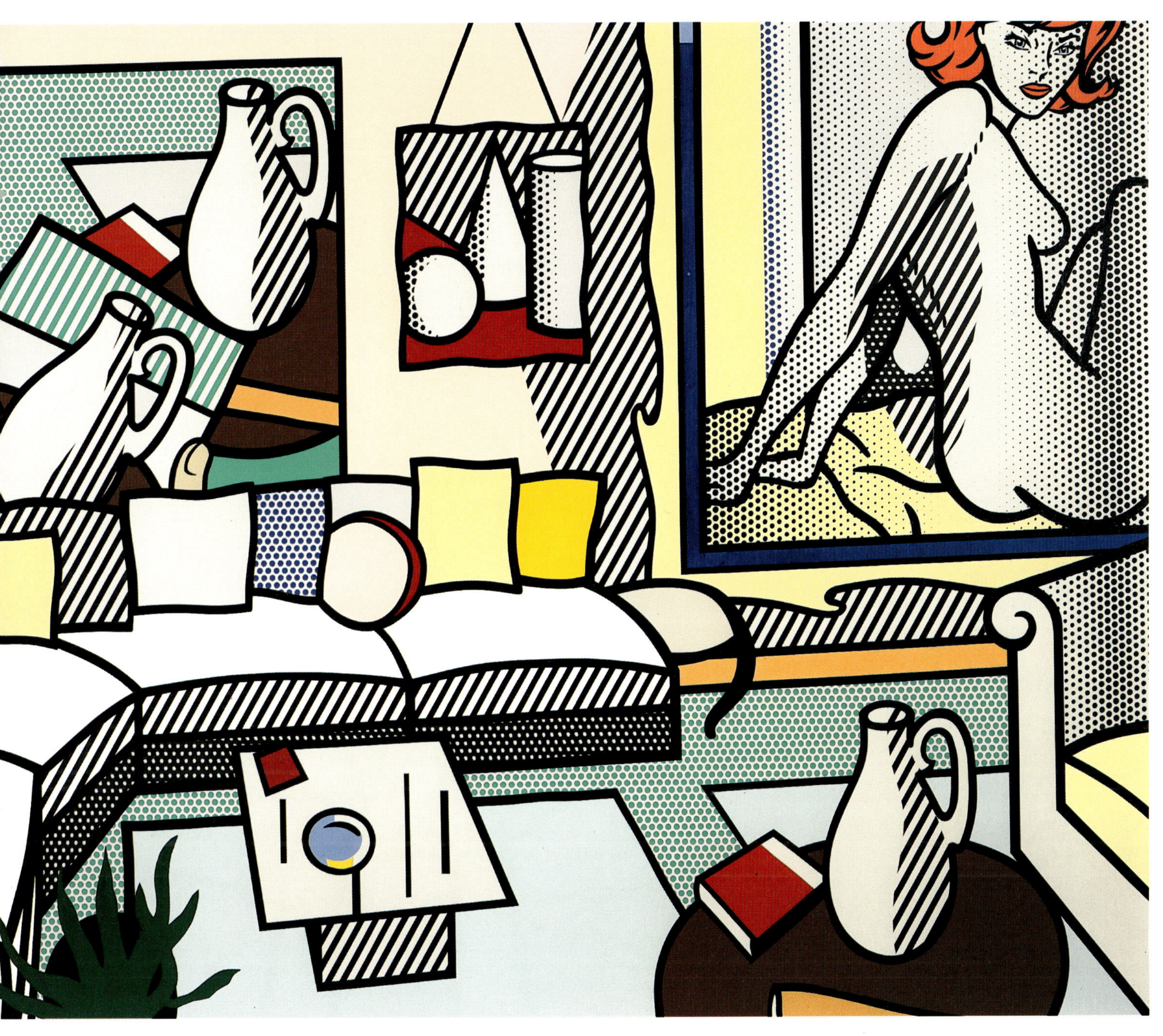

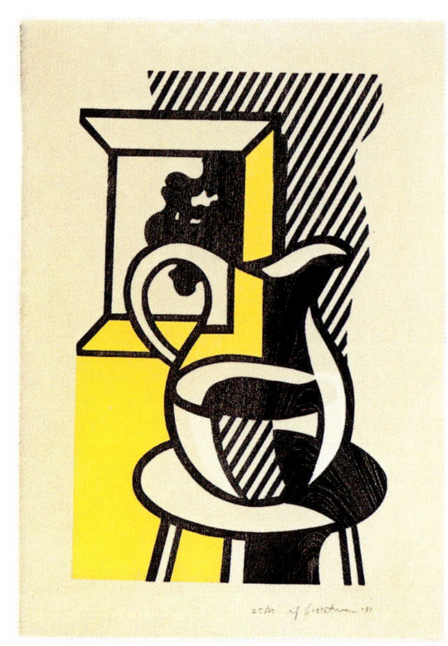

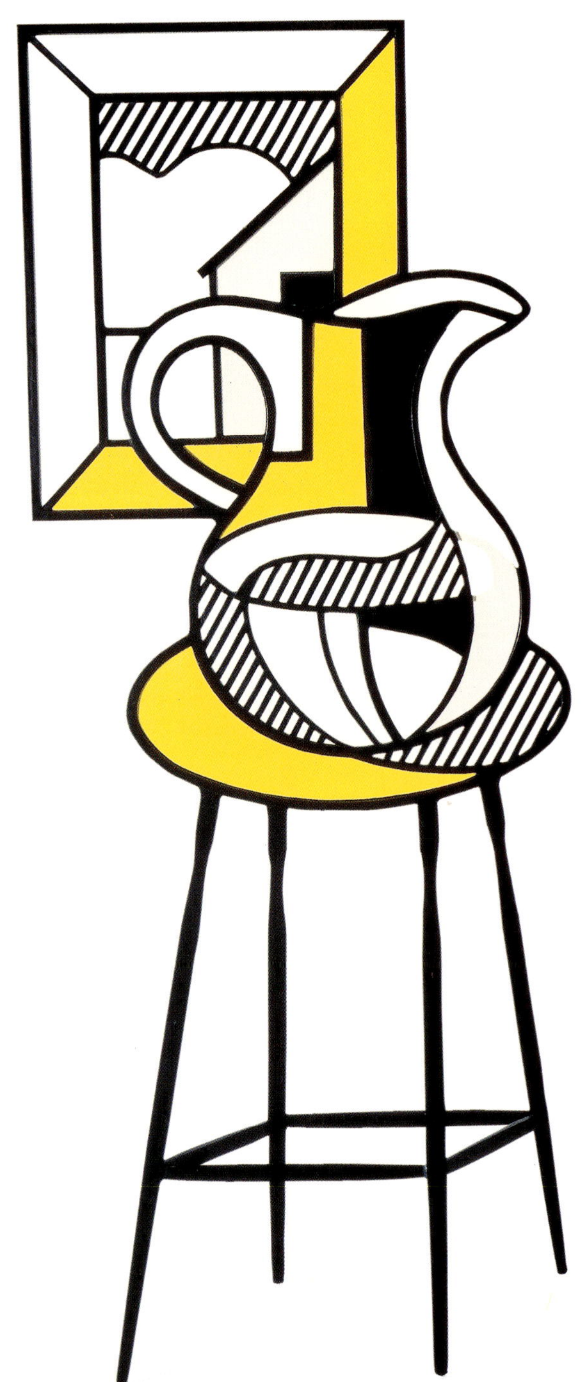

Picture and Pitcher,
1981. Cat. no. 9.

Picture and Pitcher,
1978. Cat. no. 8.

The Interior Prints

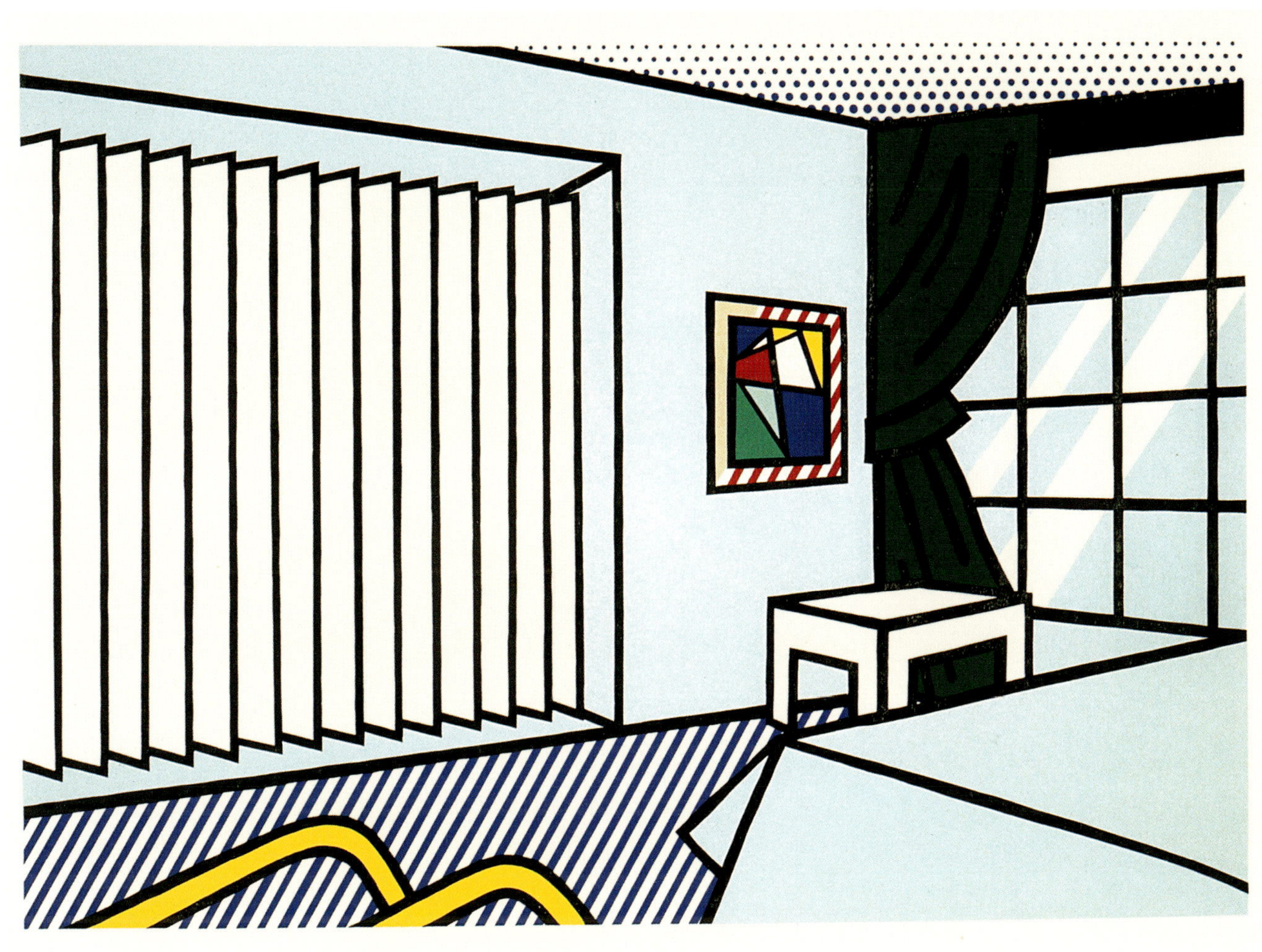

Bedroom (Gemini G.E.L. Interior Series), 1991. Cat. no. 11.

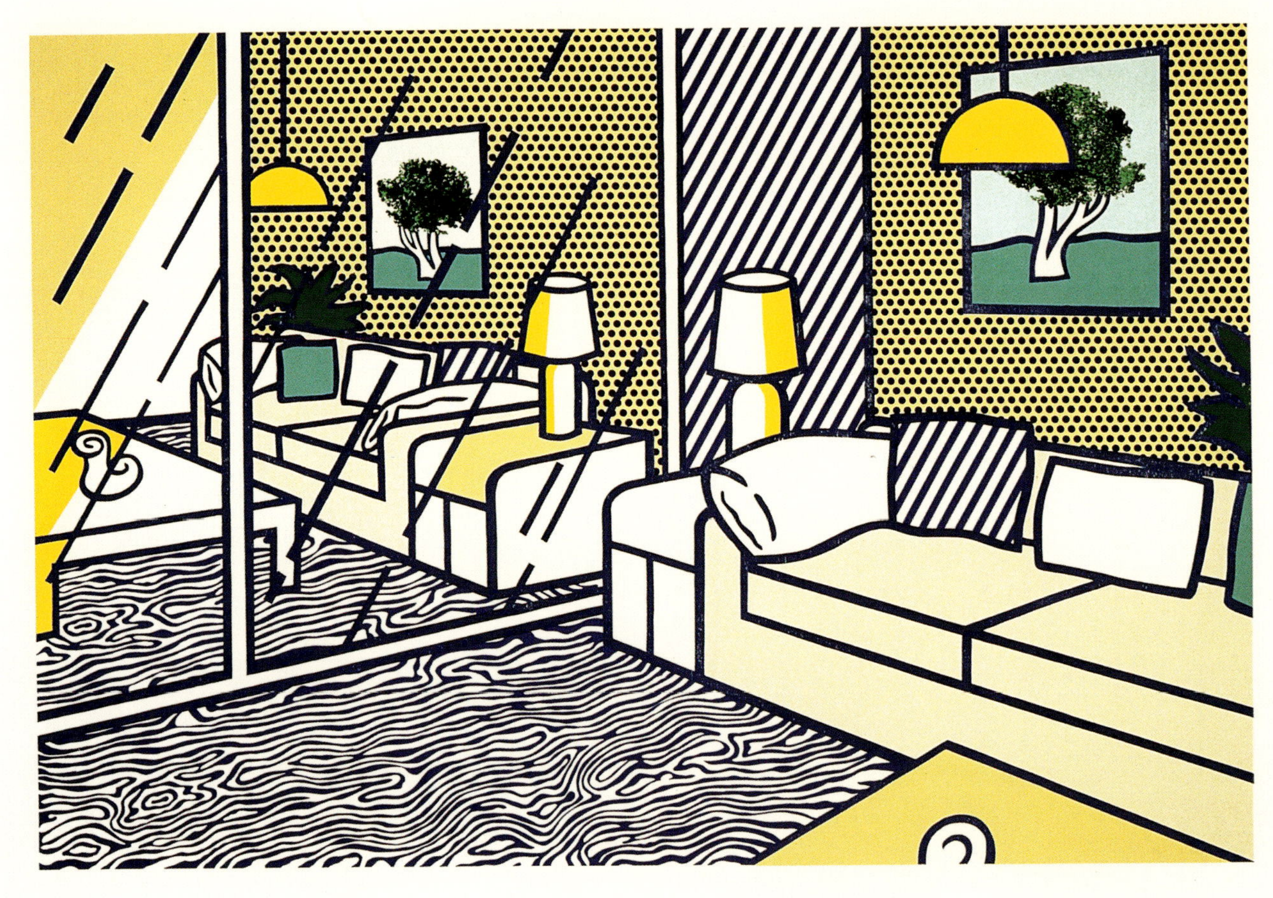

Blue Floor (Gemini G.E.L. Interior Series), 1991. Cat. no. 12.

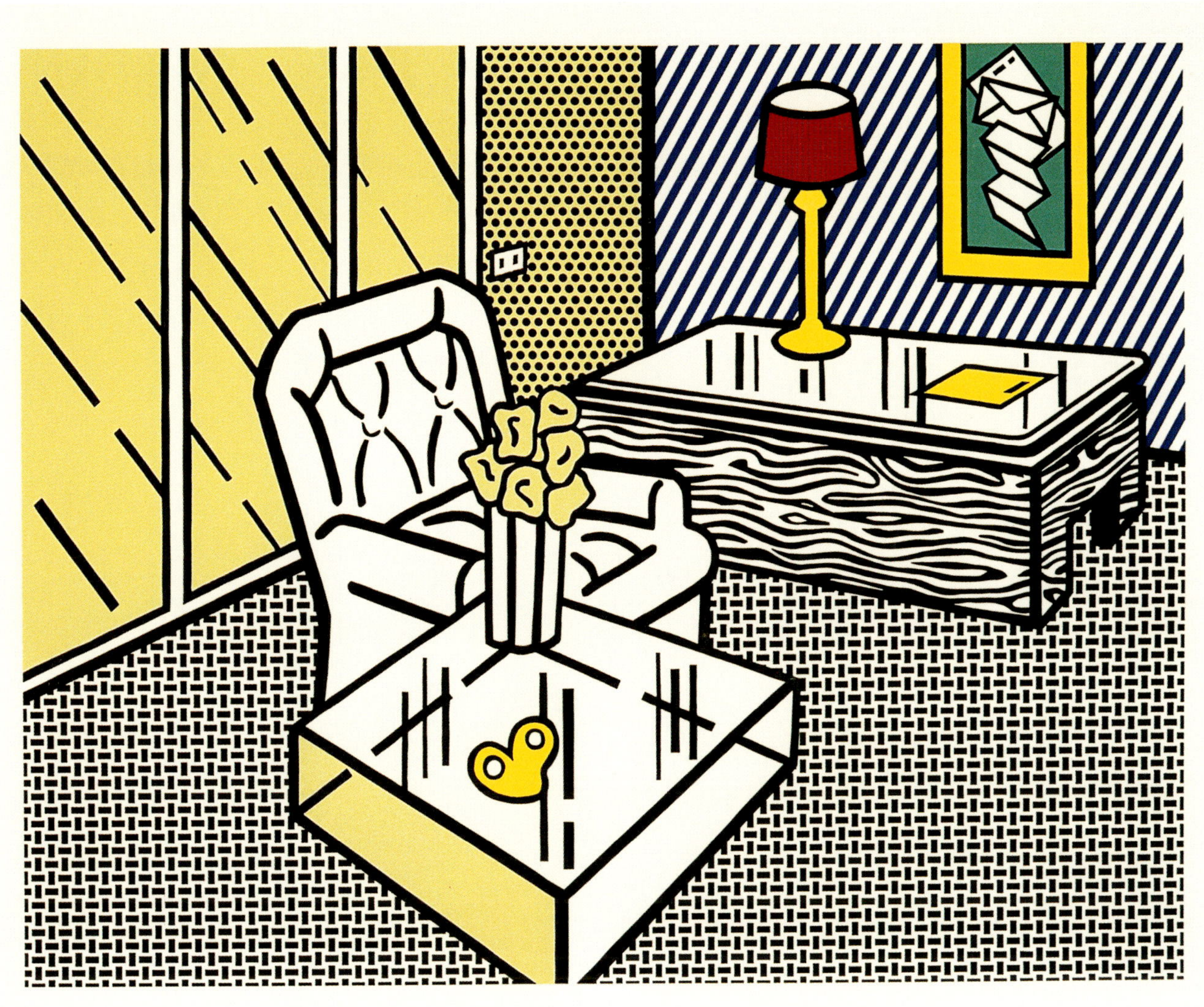

The Den (Gemini G.E.L. Interior Series), 1991. Cat. no. 13.

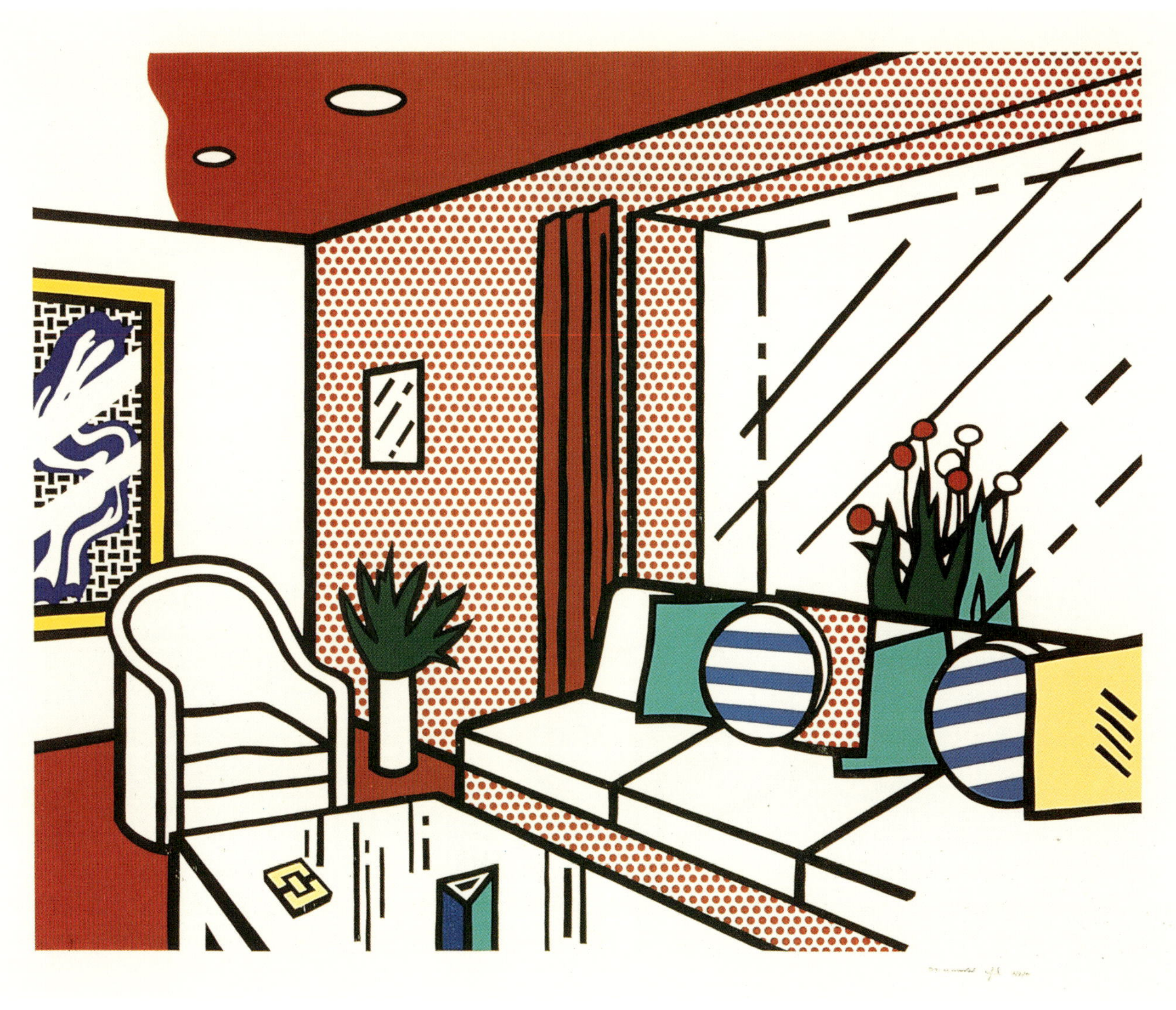

The Living Room
(Gemini G.E.L. Interior Series), 1991.
Cat. no. 21.

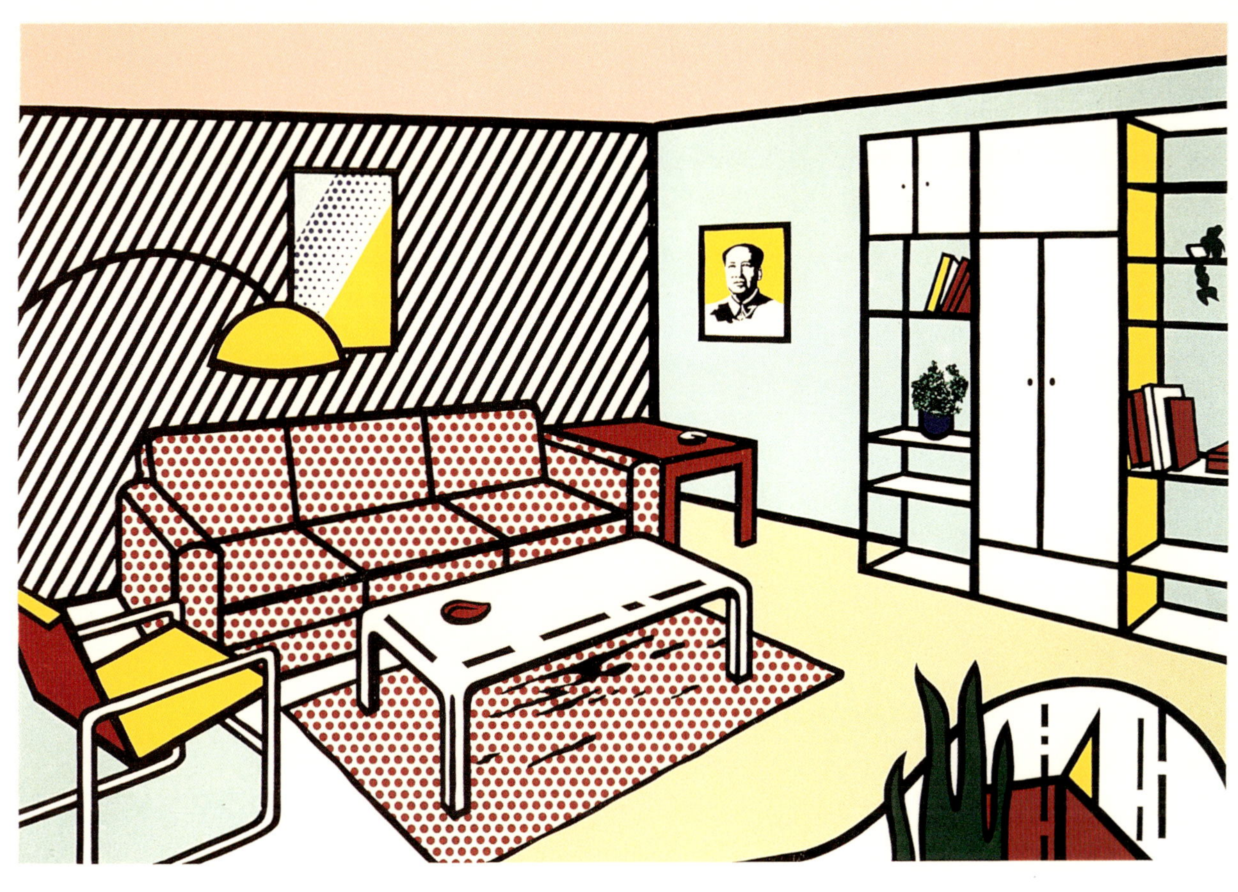

Modern Room
(Gemini G.E.L. Interior Series), 1991.
Cat. no. 22.

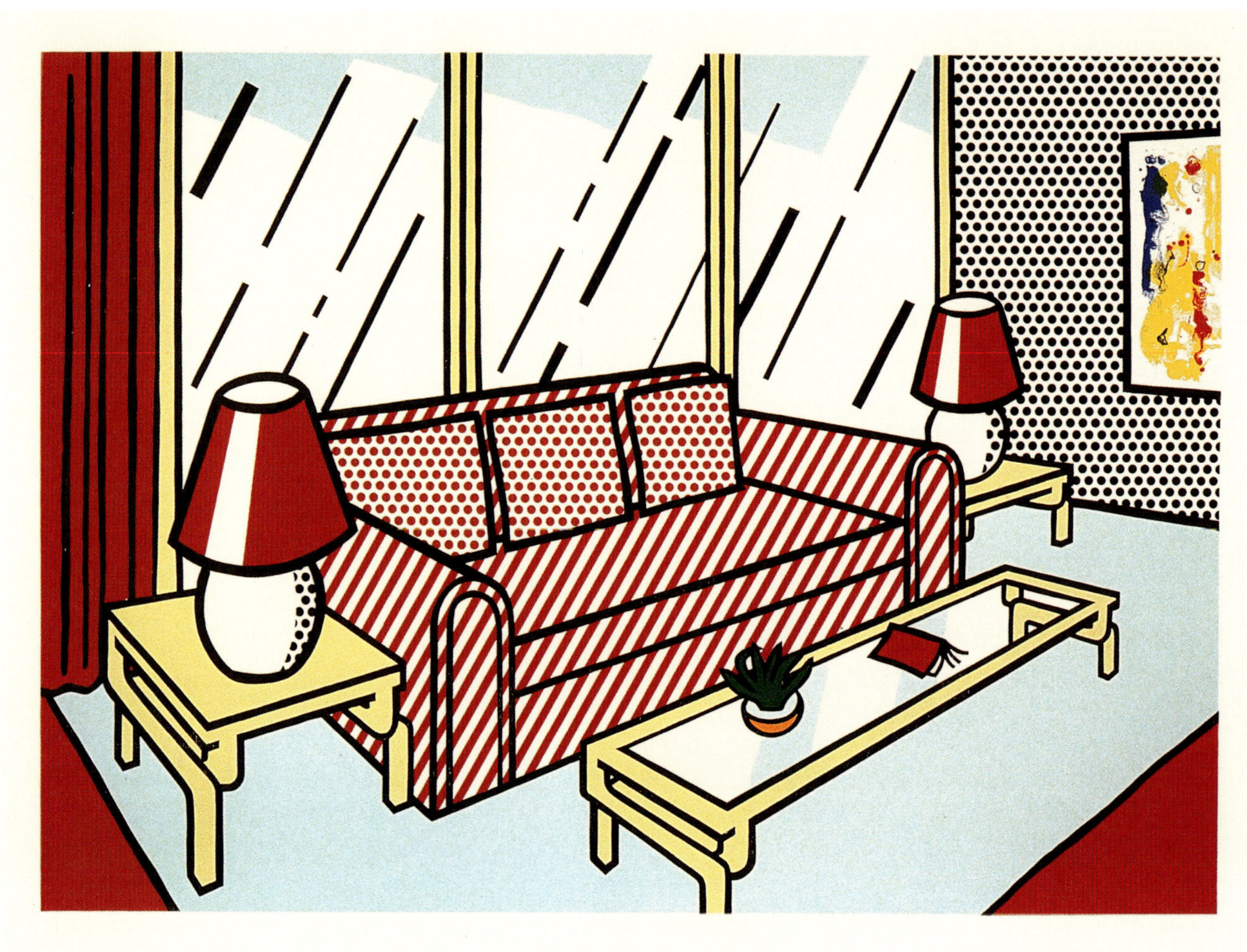

Red Lamps (Gemini G.E.L. Interior Series), 1991. Cat. no. 23.

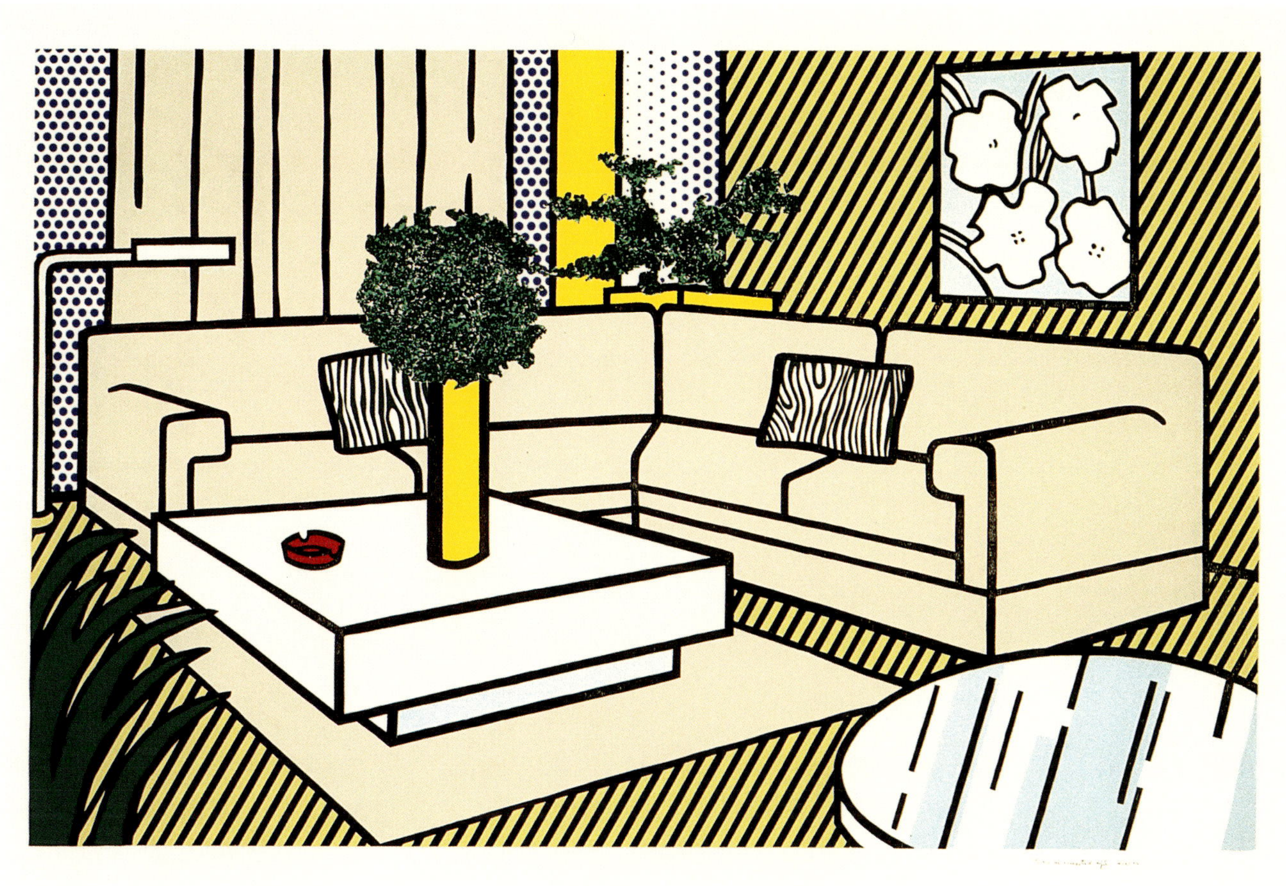

Yellow Vase (Gemini G.E.L. Interior Series), 1991. Cat. no. 25.

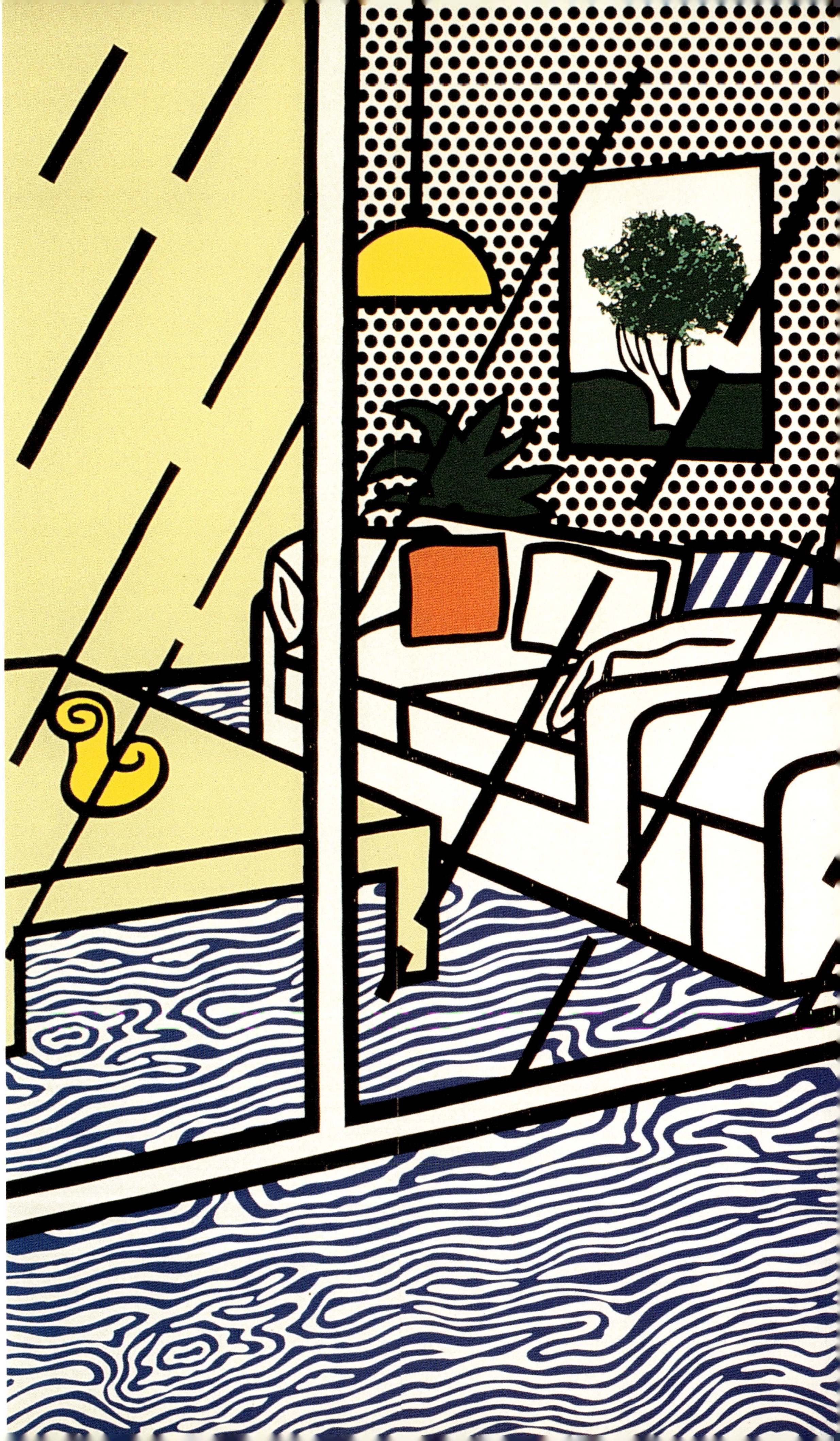

Wallpaper with Blue Floor Interior, 1992.
Cat. no. 33.

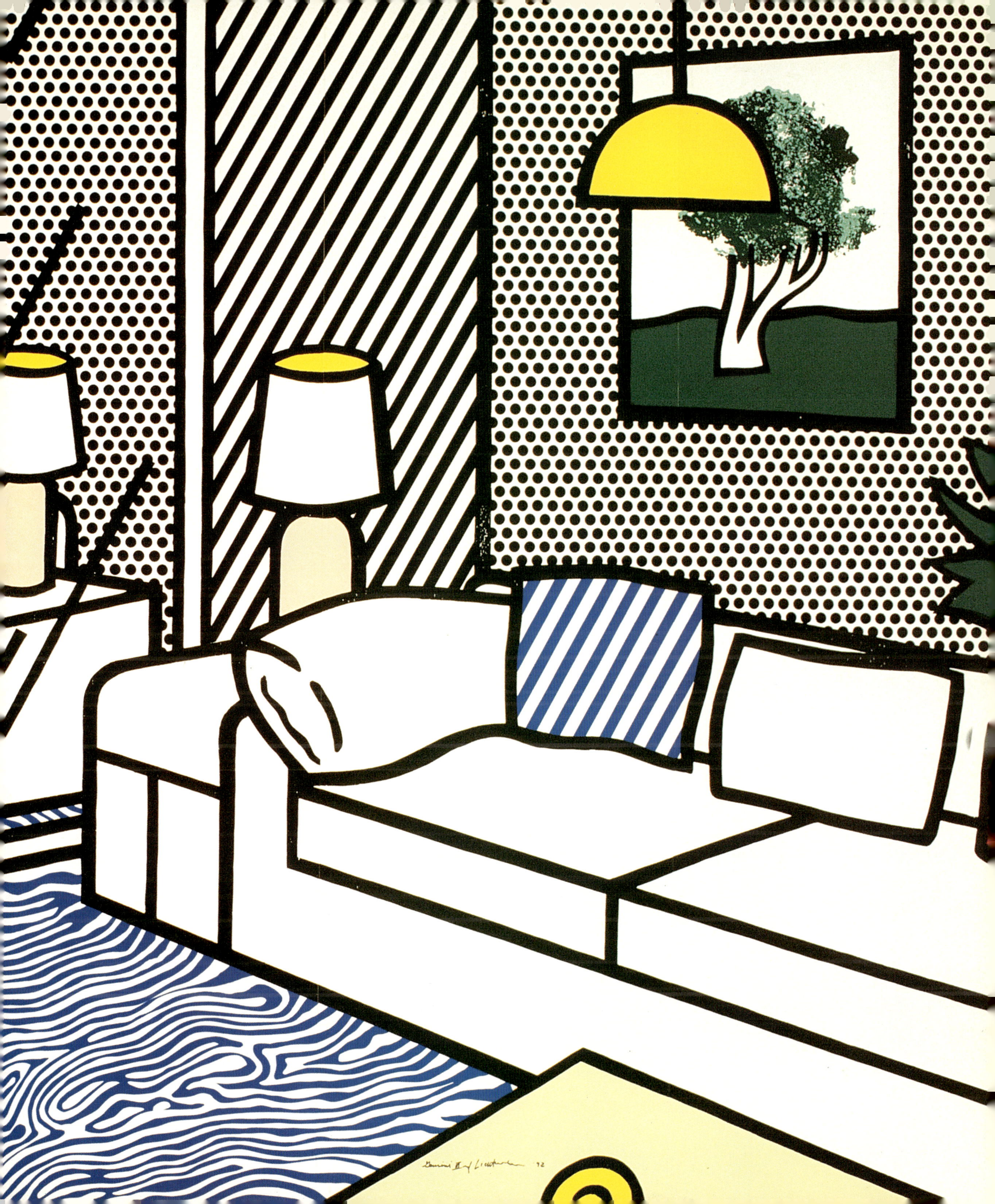

Selected Bibliography

Interviews

Enright, Robert. "Pop Goes the Tradition." *Border Crossings* 13, no. 3 (August 1994), pp. 18, 29.

Esterow, Milton. "Roy Lichtenstein: 'How Could You Be Much Luckier Than I Am?'" *Artnews* 90, no. 5 (May 1991), pp. 85–91.

Taylor, Paul. "Roy Lichtenstein." *Flash Art*, no. 148 (October 1989), pp. 87–91.

Articles, Reviews, and Books

Adams, Brooks. "New Pop Reflections." *Art in America* 80, no. 7 (July 1992), pp. 88–91.

Corlett, Mary Lee. *The Prints of Roy Lichtenstein: A Catalogue Raisonné, 1948–1993*. New York and Washington, D.C.: Hudson Hills Press in Association with the National Gallery of Art, 1994.

Camnitzer, Luis. "Marvel Entertainment Group Presents . . . " *Third Text*, no. 26 (spring 1994), pp. 99–101.

Filler, Martin. "Pop's Granddad." *Vanity Fair* (August 1993), pp. 128–34, 149–53.

Gopnik, Adam. "The Wise Innocent." *New Yorker* 69, no. 37 (8 November 1993), pp. 119–23.

Kertess, Klaus. "Roy's New Rooms." *Elle Décor* (New York) 2, no. 10 (December 1991/January 1992), pp. 56–61.

Richardson, Elizabeth. "Those Lichtenstein Women." *Harper's Bazaar* (October 1993), pp. 232–37.

Rosenthal, Mark. *Artists at Gemini G.E.L.: Celebrating the Twenty-Fifth Year*. New York and Los Angeles: Harry N. Abrams with Gemini G.E.L., 1993.

Smith, Roberta. "Inviting (If Fanciful) Rooms from the View of Roy Lichtenstein." *New York Times*, 2 June 1992, p. C23.

Wachunas, Tom. "Roy Lichtenstein." *Dialogue* 18, no. 6 (November/December 1995), p. 18.

Yood, James. "Roy Lichtenstein." *Artforum* 36, no. 8 (April 1998), p. 121.

Exhibition Catalogues

Brown, David J. *Roy Lichtenstein: Man Hit by the Twenty-First Century*. Cincinnati: Contemporary Arts Center, 1997–98.

Cowart, Jack, et al. *Roy Lichtenstein*. Monterrey, Mexico: Instituto Nacional de Bellas Artes, 1998.

Cowart, Jack. "Roy Lichtenstein: Painterly Response to Romantic Gesture," in *Roy Lichtenstein*. Basel: Fondation Beyeler, 1998. Pp. 13–20.

Francis, Richard. "Roy Lichtenstein," in *Roy Lichtenstein: Recent Drawings and Sculpture*. Chicago: Richard Gray Gallery, 1997. Pp. 3–5.

Livingstone, Marco, et al. *Pop Muses: Images of Women by Roy Lichtenstein and Andy Warhol*. Kitakyushu: Art Life Ltd., 1991.

Roy Lichtenstein: Interiors, Collages. Vienna: Galerie Ulysses, 1992.

Sylvester, David. *Some Kind of Reality: Roy Lichtenstein Interviewed by David Sylvester in 1966 and 1997*. London: Anthony D'Offay Gallery, 1997.

Waldman, Diane. "Interiors, 1991–93," in *Roy Lichtenstein*. New York: Solomon R. Guggenheim Museum, 1993. Pp. 299–311.

Video

Howard, Edgar B. *Roy Lichtenstein: Interiors*. New York: Checkerboard Film Foundation, Inc., 1993.

Howard, Edgar B., and Seth Schneider, *The Drawings of Roy Lichtenstein, 1961–1986*. New York: Checkerboard Film Foundation, Inc., 1987.

Exhibition Checklist

1. ***George Washington***, 1962
Oil and Magna on canvas
51 × 38 in.
Jean-Christophe Castelli, New York
Page 22

2. ***George Washington*** (drawing for painting), 1962
Graphite on paper
18½ × 14½ in.
Frederick W. Hughes, New York
Page 64

3. ***Oval Mirror 6' × 3' #3***, 1971
Oil and Magna on canvas
72 × 36 in.
Irving Blum Collection, New York
Pages 19 and 74

4. ***Bananas and Grapefruit I***, 1972
Oil and Magna on canvas
20 × 28 in.
Private collection, New York
Page 56

5. ***Pitcher Triptych***, 1972
Oil and Magna on canvas
30 × 72 in.
Private collection, courtesy Gallery Beyeler
Pages 20–21

6. ***Artist's Studio: Model*** (drawing for painting), 1974
Graphite and colored pencil on paper
19½ × 24¼ in.
Private collection, New York
Page 26

7. ***Untitled*** (drawing), 1976
Graphite and colored pencil on paper
9 × 7 in.
Private collection
Page 67

8. ***Picture and Pitcher***, 1978
Polyurethane enamel and Magna on bronze
95 × 40 × 24½ in.
Albright-Knox Art Gallery, Buffalo, N.Y.; Edmund Hayes and Charles Clifton Funds, 1978
Page 84

9. ***Picture and Pitcher***, 1981
Woodcut on handmade Okawara paper
25 × 18½ in.
Private collection, New York
Page 84

10. ***Untitled*** (drawing), 1989
Graphite and colored pencil on paper
7½ × 11 in.
Stefan T. Edlis Collection, Chicago
Page 40

11. ***Bedroom*** (Gemini G.E.L. Interior Series), 1991
Color woodcut and screenprint on board
56¾ × 78½ in.
Gemini G.E.L., Los Angeles
Page 87

12. ***Blue Floor*** (Gemini G.E.L. Interior Series), 1991
Color lithograph, woodcut, and screenprint on board
57¾ × 83½ in.
Gemini G.E.L., Los Angeles
Page 88

13. ***The Den*** (Gemini G.E.L. Interior Series), 1991
Color woodcut and screenprint on board
57½ × 71½ in.
Gemini G.E.L., Los Angeles
Page 89

14. ***Interior with African Mask***, 1991
Oil and Magna on canvas
114 × 146 in.
The Eli and Edythe L. Broad Collection, Los Angeles
Pages 72–73, 75, and 77

15. ***Interior with African Mask*** (collage for painting), 1991
Printed paper and Magna on board
39 × 48¾ in.
Private collection, New York
Page 72

16. ***Interior with Bonsai Tree***, 1991
Oil and Magna on canvas
118 × 140 in.
Private collection, New York
Pages 44–45 and 47

17. ***Interior with Bonsai Tree***
(drawing for painting), 1991
Graphite on polyester
tracing film
26 1/4 × 35 1/4 in.
Jerald Ordover Collection
Page 44

18. ***Interior with Exterior (Still Waters)***, 1991
Oil and Magna on canvas
102 × 173 in.
Gagosian Gallery, New York
Pages 62–63

19. ***Interior with Exterior (Still Waters)***
(drawing for painting), 1991
Graphite on paper
6 × 5 1/2 in.
Robert and Trina McKeever,
New York
Page 64

20. ***Interior with Exterior (Still Waters)***
(collage for painting), 1991
Printed paper and Magna
on board
33 × 51 in.
Private collection, New York
Page 65

21. ***The Living Room*** (Gemini G.E.L.
Interior Series), 1991
Color woodcut and
screenprint on board
58 × 72 in.
Gemini G.E.L., Los Angeles
Page 90

22. ***Modern Room*** (Gemini G.E.L.
Interior Series), 1991
Color lithograph, woodcut,
and screenprint on board
56 × 80 3/4 in.
Gemini G.E.L., Los Angeles
Page 91

23. ***Red Lamps*** (Gemini G.E.L.
Interior Series), 1991
Color lithograph, woodcut, and
screenprint on board
57 1/4 × 78 3/4 in.
Gemini G.E.L., Los Angeles
Page 92

24. ***La Sortie*** (Gemini G.E.L.
Interior Series), 1991
Color woodcut on board
58 1/2 × 81 in.
Gemini G.E.L., Los Angeles
Page 28

25. ***Yellow Vase*** (Gemini G.E.L. Interior Series), 1991
Color lithograph, woodcut, and
screenprint on board
55 1/2 × 84 1/2 in.
Gemini G.E.L., Los Angeles
Page 93

26. ***Bonsai Tree***, 1992
Polyurethane enamel and Magna
on cast pewter, and patinated cast
bronze
51 × 43 × 10 1/2 in.
Private collection, New York
Page 46

27. ***Bonsai Tree***
(drawing for sculpture), 1992
Graphite on paper
9 × 6 in.
Private collection, New York
Page 46

28. ***Chair, Table, and Flower Pot***
(maquette for sculpture), 1992
Tape, printed paper, and
Magna on Foamcore
22 × 50 × 11 1/4 in.
Private collection, New York
Page 67

29. ***Interior with Motel Room Painting***, 1992
Oil and Magna on canvas
77 × 96 in.
Private collection, New York
Page 41

30. ***Interior with Motel Room Painting***
(drawing for painting), 1992
Graphite and colored pencil
on paper
6 3/4 × 10 in.
Private collection,
La Jolla, California
Page 40

31. ***Ritual Mask***, 1992
Polyurethane enamel and Magna
on galvanized steel
51 × 26 1/2 × 11 1/2 in.
Private collection, New York
Page 76

32. ***Ritual Mask***
(study for sculpture), 1992
Graphite on paper
6 × 4 in.
Private collection, New York
Page 76

33. ***Wallpaper with Blue Floor Interior***, 1992
Screenprint on Waterleaf paper
102 × 150 in.
102 × 30½ in. (each sheet)
Museum of Contemporary Art, Chicago
Gift of Richard Gray Gallery
Pages 94–95

34. ***Chair, Table, and Flower Pot***, 1993
Polyurethane enamel and Magna on cast bronze
63 × 153 × 35 in.
Private collection, New York
Pages 66–67

35. ***Idea***, 1993
Oil and Magna on canvas
90 × 61 in.
Private collection, New York
Page 81

36. ***Idea*** (sketch for painting), 1993
Graphite and colored pencil on paper
9¾ × 6¾ in.
Private collection, New York
Pages 24 and 80

37. ***Idea*** (drawing for painting), 1993
Graphite and colored pencil on paper
9¾ × 6¾ in.
Private collection, New York
Page 80

38. ***Interior with T'aime*** (collage for painting), 1993
Printed paper and Magna on board
31½ × 49½ in.
Private collection, New York
Page 39

39. ***Interior with T'aime*** (drawing for painting), 1993
Graphite on paper
3½ × 5 in.
David and Marjorie Silverman, New York
Page 35

40. ***Large Interior with Three Reflections***, 1993
Oil and Magna on canvas
137 × 367¾ in.
111¼ × 79¾ in. (left panel)
111¼ × 88¾ in. (center panel)
111¼ × 79¾ in. (right panel)
Revlon Collection, New York
Pages 51–54, 57, 59, and 61

41. ***Large Interior with Three Reflections*** (drawings for painting), 1993
Graphite and colored pencil on paper
16¼ × 30 in. (left)
15 × 24¼ in. (right)
Private collection, New York
Pages 50 and 55

42. ***Large Interior with Three Reflections***, ***Interior with T'aime***, *and* ***Cityscape*** (sketches for paintings and sculpture), 1993
Graphite on paper
9¾ × 6¾ in.
Private collection, New York
Pages 38 and 56

43. ***Large Interior with Three Reflections*** (sketch for painting), 1993
Graphite on tracing paper
4 × 10 in.
Private collection, New York
Pages 11 and 56

44. ***Interior with T'aime***, 1994
Oil and Magna on canvas
110½ × 168 in.
Charles Simonyi, Medina, Washington
Pages 36–37

45. ***Interior: Perfect Pitcher***, 1994
Oil and Magna on canvas
120 × 193¾ in.
Private collection, New York
Pages 82–83

46. ***Interior: Perfect Pitcher*** (drawing for painting), 1994
Graphite and colored pencil on paper
6¾ × 4½ in.
Private collection, New York
Page 82

47. ***Interior: Perfect Pitcher*** (sketch for painting), 1994
Graphite on paper
$9\frac{3}{4} \times 6\frac{3}{4}$ in.
Private collection, New York

48. ***Nude with Yellow Flower***, 1994
Oil and Magna on canvas
92 × 72 in.
Stefan T. Edlis Collection, Chicago
Cover and page 43

49. ***Blue Nude***, 1995
Oil and Magna on canvas
81 × 60 in.
Private collection
Page 79

50. ***Cityscape***, 1995
Polyurethane enamel and Magna on cast stainless steel
$36\frac{3}{4} \times 13\frac{1}{2} \times 11$ in.
Private collection, New York
Page 56

51. ***Endless Drip***, 1995
Polyurethane enamel on aluminum
$147\frac{1}{4} \times 27\frac{1}{2} \times 27\frac{1}{2}$ in.
Private collection, New York
Page 70

52. ***Imperfect Sculpture***, 1995
Stained cast iron, polyurethane enamel, and Magna on stainless steel and wood
$30\frac{3}{4} \times 34\frac{3}{4} \times 5$ in.
Private collection, New York
Pages 38 and 60

53. ***Nude With Bust***, 1995
Oil and Magna on canvas
108 × 90 in.
Private collection, New York
Page 71

54. ***Nude with Bust*** (collage for painting), 1995
Tape, printed paper, and Magna on board
54 × 45 in.
Private collection, New York
Page 69

55. ***Nude with Bust*** (drawing for painting), 1995
Graphite and colored pencil on polyester tracing film
$15\frac{1}{2} \times 9\frac{1}{2}$ in.
Private collection, New York
Page 68

56. ***Nude with Bust*** (sketch for painting), 1995
Graphite on tracing paper
$8\frac{1}{2} \times 5\frac{1}{4}$ in.
Private collection, New York
Page 70

57. ***Nude with Bust*** (drawing for painting), 1995
Graphite and colored pencil on paper
$10 \times 8\frac{1}{4}$ in.
Private collection, New York
Page 68

58. ***House I*** (full-scale maquette for sculpture), 1996
Polyurethane enamel and Magna on wood
124 × 201 × 44 in.
Private collection, New York

59. ***Woman: Sunlight, Moonlight***, 1996
Polyurethane enamel and Magna on patinated bronze
$39\frac{1}{2} \times 25\frac{1}{4} \times 16\frac{1}{2}$ in.
Private collection, New York
Page 70

60. ***House I*** (maquette for sculpture), 1997
Tape, printed paper, and Magna on Foamcore
$13\frac{1}{2} \times 22\frac{1}{2} \times 5\frac{1}{4}$ in.
Private collection, New York
Page 49

61. ***House with Gray Roof***, 1997
Graphite and colored pencil on paper
$8 \times 8\frac{3}{4}$ in.
Richard Gray Gallery, Chicago and New York
Page 48

62. ***Interior with Bouquet***, 1997
Graphite and colored pencil on paper
$8 \times 8\frac{3}{4}$ in.
Richard Gray Gallery, Chicago and New York
Frontispiece

Lenders to the Exhibition

Albright-Knox Art Gallery, Buffalo, N.Y.

Mary Beebe and Charles Reilly

Private collection, courtesy Gallery Beyeler

Irving Blum Collection

The Eli and Edythe L. Broad Collection

Jean-Christophe Castelli

Stefan T. Edlis Collection

Gagosian Gallery, New York

Gemini G.E.L.

Richard Gray Gallery, Chicago and New York

Agnes Gund

Frederick W. Hughes

Estate of Roy Lichtenstein

Jeffrey Loria

Robert and Trina McKeever

Jerald Ordover Collection

Revlon Collection

David and Marjorie Silverman

Charles Simonyi

United Yarn Products Company, Inc.

Versace Group

Notes on Contributors

LEO CASTELLI (1907–1999) was born in Trieste. He moved to New York in 1941, and served in the United States Army Intelligence Corps during World War II. Since 1957, when he opened his art gallery in New York, he has been one of the most significant figures in contemporary art. Among the artists he has represented are Jasper Johns, Roy Lichtenstein, Robert Rauschenberg, Frank Stella, Cy Twombly, and Andy Warhol.

SIDNEY B. FELSEN is cofounder and Director of Gemini G.E.L., an artists' workshop and publisher of limited editions of graphics and sculpture. Since 1966, many of the most important contemporary artists have worked at Gemini and formed close relationships with him. His photographs of these artists have been reproduced and exhibited widely.

ROBERT FITZPATRICK is Director of the Museum of Contemporary Art, Chicago. From 1995 to 1998, he was Dean of the School of the Arts at Columbia University. He has also been President and Chief Executive Officer of EuroDisney, Director of the 1984 Olympic Arts Festival in Los Angeles, President of the California Institute of the Arts, and Dean of Students at Johns Hopkins University.

DOROTHY LICHTENSTEIN met Roy Lichtenstein when she was organizing the 1964 exhibition *The Great American Supermarket* at the Bianchini Gallery, in which he participated. They were married in 1968. She was actively involved in the artist's work until his death in 1997, and she is President of the Roy Lichtenstein Foundation.

CASSANDRA LOZANO began to work for Roy Lichtenstein in 1990, managing his studio and establishing the first comprehensive archive of his work. She is currently the Managing Director of the Roy Lichtenstein Foundation. Her paintings, drawings, and sculptural frames have been exhibited in numerous galleries and in a solo exhibition in 1998 at The Andy Warhol Museum in Pittsburgh.

Photography Credits

Unless otherwise indicated in the captions, illustrations were provided by the following:

Estate of Roy Lichtenstein:
Robert McKeever
Cover, frontispiece, and pages 8, 15–17, 23, 25, 35–37, 38 (fig. 4), 39, 40 (bottom), 41, 43–45, 46 (fig. 1), 47–49, 51–54, 56 (fig. 2), 57, 58 (fig. 2), 59, 60 (fig. 2), 61–63, 64 (fig. 2), 65–66, 70 (figs. 1–2), 71–73, 74 (fig. 1), 75, 76 (fig. 1), 77, 79, 80 (fig. 2), 81, 82 (fig. 1), and 83

Estate of Roy Lichtenstein:
Kevin Ryan
Back cover and pages 11, 24, 29, 38 (fig. 2–3), 42, 46 (figs. 2–4), 50, 55, 56 (figs. 1 and 3–8), 58 (figs. 1 and 4), 60 (figs. 1 and 3), 64 (fig. 4), 67–70, 70 (figs. 3–4 and 8), 74 (fig. 4), 76 (figs. 2–3), 78, 80 (figs. 1 and 3–5), and 82 (figs. 2–4)

Zindman/Fremont
Pages 19 and 74 (fig. 2)

Fondation Beyeler, Riehen/Basel
Pages 20–21

Eric Pollitzer
Page 22

Kate Keller, The Museum of Modern Art, New York
Page 26

Roy Lichtenstein/Gemini G.E.L., Los Angeles © 1991
Pages 28 and 87–95

Philipp Scholz Rittermann
Page 40 (top)

Frederick Hughes
Page 64 (fig. 3)

Stephen Ogilvy, New York
Page 84 (bottom)

Colophon

The type for this catalogue was set in Scala and Scala Sans. Designed by Martin Majoor for the Vredenburg concert hall in Utrecht, these neohumanist typefaces were issued publicly by FontShop International, Berlin, in 1991 and 1994, respectively.

This catalogue was printed by Cantz in Germany on Luxosamtoffset paper. The color separations were created by Professional Graphics in Rockford, Illinois.